If I could only recommend one book to a teacher asking how to engage students in deeper learning, I would recommend this one—again and again!

—Patti Castellano, executive director for curriculum and instruction, North East ISD, San Antonio, Texas

I thought that the first edition of *Total Participation Techniques* was a "must-read" book for teachers. The Himmeles have made a great book even better with this second edition!

—Larry Ferlazzo, teacher, *Ed Week* teacher advice columnist, author

Total Participation Techniques, 2nd ed., is a must have for teachers at all levels. The ideas presented here will help you take your students' thinking to new depths and your teaching to new heights.

—Rose Cappelli, coauthor of *Mentor Texts* *Nonfiction Mentor Texts*, and *Poetry Mentor Texts*

I can't say enough good things about how useful and practical this book is: the Himmeles have made it so much simpler for teachers to observe growth as it happens and celebrate students' learning.

—Angela Watson, author of "Unshakeable" and creator of The 40 Hour Teacher Workweek Club

This book provides a deep dive into strategies and how to implement them for impactful cognitive engagement. It is a superb, research-based professional development tool and a must-have for teachers and instructional leaders!

—Dr. Nancy A. Aronson, retired principal NAESP Certified Principal Mentor

I found myself taking feverish notes as I am excited by some of the new ideas that I will share with my staff! This teacher-friendly second edition offers more TPT strategies for instructors to add to their 'bag of tricks' to increase students' cognitive engagement.

—Kimberly Stoltz, principal, Yorkshire Elementary York Suburban School District, PA

The TPTs in this book will help you change the way you teach and your expectations, providing you opportunities to truly understand your students' capabilities, becoming a more effective, intentional and empowered educator.

—Rosemarie Zorrilla, World Languages/ESL supervisor Hempfield School District, Landisville, PA

TOTAL Participation
Techniques 2nd Edition

ASCD MEMBER BOOK

Many ASCD members received this book as a
member benefit upon its initial release.

Learn more at: **www.ascd.org/memberbooks**

Other ASCD publications by the authors

*The Language-Rich Classroom: A Research-Based Framework
for Teaching English Language Learners*
by Pérsida Himmele and William Himmele

*Total Literacy Techniques: Tools to Help Students Analyze
Literature and Informational Texts*
by Pérsida Himmele, William Himmele, and Keely Potter

*Total Participation Techniques to Engage Students:
Quick Reference Guide*
by Pérsida Himmele and William Himmele

**Select items from this book are available
for download at this URL:
www.ascd.org/ASCD/pdf/books/himmele2017.pdf**

TOTAL Participation Techniques

Making Every Student an Active Learner

2nd Edition

Pérsida Himmele

William Himmele

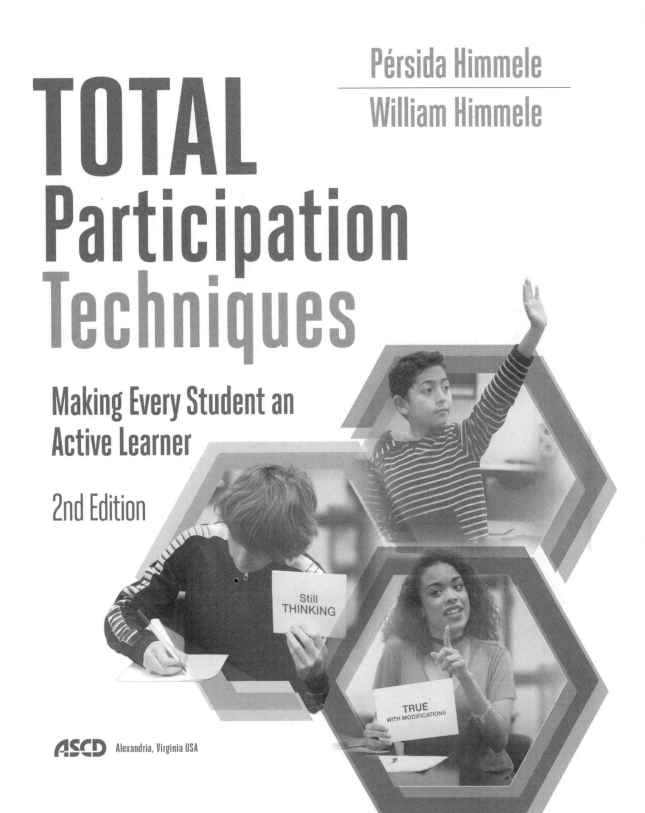

Still THINKING

TRUE
WITH MODIFICATIONS

ASCD Alexandria, Virginia USA

1703 N. Beauregard St. • Alexandria, VA 22311-1714 USA
Phone: 800-933-2723 or 703-578-9600 • Fax: 703-575-5400
Website: www.ascd.org • E-mail: member@ascd.org
Author guidelines: www.ascd.org/write

Deborah S. Delisle, *Executive Director;* Robert D. Clouse, *Managing Director, Digital Content & Publications;* Stefani Roth, *Publisher;* Genny Ostertag, *Director, Content Acquisitions;* Julie Houtz, *Director, Book Editing & Production;* Darcie Russell, *Senior Associate Editor;* Georgia Park, *Senior Graphic Designer;* Mike Kalyan, *Director, Production Services;* Keith Demmons, *Production Designer;* Kelly Marshall, *Senior Production Specialist*

All web links in this book are correct as of the publication date below but may have become inactive or otherwise modified since that time. If you notice a deactivated or changed link, please e-mail books@ascd.org with the words "Link Update" in the subject line. In your message, please specify the web link, the book title, and the page number on which the link appears.

ASCD Member Book No. FY17-8B (July 2017 PS). Member books mail to Premium (P), Select (S), and Institutional Plus (I+) members on this schedule: Jan, PSI+; Feb, P; Apr, PSI+; May, P; Jul, PSI+; Aug, P; Sep, PSI+; Nov, PSI+; Dec, P. For details, see www.ascd.org/membership and www.ascd.org/memberbooks.

PAPERBACK ISBN: 978-1-4166-2399-1   ASCD product: 117033
PDF E-BOOK ISBN: 978-1-4166-2401-1; see Books in Print for other formats.
Quantity discounts are available: e-mail programteam@ascd.org or call 800-933-2723, ext. 5773, or 703-575-5773. For desk copies, go to www.ascd.org/deskcopy.

Library of Congress Cataloging-in-Publication Data

Names: Himmele, Pérsida, author. | Himmele, William, author.
Title: Total participation techniques : making every student an active learner / Pérsida Himmele and William Himmele.
Description: Second edition. | Alexandria, Virginia : ASCD, [2017] | Includes bibliographical references and index.
Identifiers: LCCN 2017017381 (print) | LCCN 2017010667 (ebook) | ISBN 9781416623991 (pbk.) | ISBN 9781416624011 (PDF)
Subjects: LCSH: Active learning. | Creative teaching.
Classification: LCC LB1027.23 .H56 2017 (ebook) | LCC LB1027.23 (print) | DDC 371.1--dc23
LC record available at https://lccn.loc.gov/2017017381

26 25 24 23 22 21 20 19 18   3 4 5 6 7 8 9 10 11 12

This book is dedicated to our dear friend, Keely Potter, who has made such a difference in the lives of the many children she taught, and who continues to make a difference through her leadership role at the state level in Tennessee.

TOTAL Participation Techniques 2nd Edition

Making Every Student an Active Learner

Acknowledgments

We would like to acknowledge the friends and colleagues who have helped bring this book to completion, as well as those who have shaped our thinking along the way. We want to thank Genny Ostertag, acquisitions editor, who helped us refine the topic for the first edition of this book, and who later supported us through the proposal and writing stage of the second edition. We also want to thank Darcie Russell, our project manager, who has been a joy to work with and whose perceptive eye was so helpful in producing this second edition. And Georgia Park, senior graphic designer, and Kevin Davis, lead photographer, did fabulous work in making this book visually appealing and supporting the effectiveness of the text. We'd like to thank Stefani Roth, publisher, and Laura Lawson and Deborah Siegel, who worked on the first edition and gave this book a great start. And we'd like to thank Julie Huggins, who did a great job improving and fine-tuning our accompanying TPT Quick Reference Guide. We have always felt that ASCD produces high-quality work, and we are proud to be among its authors.

We'd like to thank Keely Potter, a dear friend, a gifted teacher, and currently Director of Teacher Effectiveness at the Tennessee Department of Education. She has had a lasting impression on the lives of those whom she has taught, as well as on us. Keely doesn't just teach the mind—she touches hearts. We are indebted to Keely for demonstrating the Total Participation Techniques and for scouting out great teachers who could provide us with real-life examples for this book.

We are indebted to Karen Hess and the Manheim Central School District administration in south-central Pennsylvania for allowing us to work alongside eight fabulous teachers. We also want to thank the Manheim Central Middle School teachers: Meghan Babcock, Matt Baker, Courtney Cislo,

Liz Lubeskie, Shannon Paules, Keely Potter, Mike Pyle, and Julie Wash. We witnessed some amazing teaching and heard their passion for teaching and learning come through in their interviews. They demonstrated a commitment to continuously sharpen their craft, a commitment that should make them and their district very proud. Additional teachers who modeled TPT lessons for accompanying resources include Melanie Upton and Doreen Hershey from Conestoga Valley High School; and Krista Grimm, Susan Hagel, and Quirine Gladwish from Washington Elementary School. Thanks also to Beth Ferguson, author of the blog Algebra's Friend, and Heather Berrier, a former student teacher, for allowing us to feature one of their lessons in our book. We'd like to thank Jennifer Schnabel, Mary Iovino, Marie Grutza, and Dr. Carmen Rowe for their critical and honest feedback on this second edition. We'd also like to thank administrators Michelle Trasborg (Conestoga Valley School District), Arthur Paynter (Manheim Central School District), Dr. Nancy Aronson (West Chester Area School District), and Dr. Margie Sharp (Avon Grove School District), who have supported us throughout this work by inviting us into their schools.

Appreciation and thanks to our many workshop participants and college students, whose feedback (either by way of droopy eyes or high fives) taught us the importance of TPTs at every age. And we want to thank our families, parents, and siblings, who have taught us that a good education leads to vocational choice and freedom, and that being at the center of education can help us directly and indirectly be the answer to the prayers of a parent's heart for his or her child.

A very special thanks to our children, Gabriela and Caleb, who are always in the center of our minds when we write. Thanks for keeping us grounded in what matters to kids.

Finally, the more we study cognition, the more humbled and grateful we are for the complexities of the human brain. As people of faith, we are increasingly thankful to God for his eloquent and indescribable gift of life and the ability to know more deeply. We really have been fearfully and wonderfully made, and we see God's hand in the science of learning.

Introduction

Have you ever noticed how teachers react to the type of professional development seminars known as "stand and deliver"? By "stand and deliver," we certainly don't mean the Jaime Escalante movie about improving students' understanding of mathematics. We mean the type of teaching that occurs when presenters stand and deliver long, drawn-out presentations in lecture style. The next time you're a recipient of this type of presentation, look around and observe your peers. Most likely some of them have their laptops open and are reading or writing e-mail messages, posting on social media, or texting friends; others are openly chattering away; and some are quietly heading for another cup of coffee just to maintain their respectful composure. All this goes on while the speaker drones on and on.

Whereas adults have discovered activity-based coping mechanisms, children don't have that luxury. Although some students will find ways to become *actively* disengaged, many are respectfully but *passively* disengaged. Many aren't allowed to carry cell phones or laptops, and most aren't allowed to chatter away in class. Many children have learned to cope by simply following the teacher with their eyes. Often they're sitting on the periphery of the classroom, looking at the teacher, but in reality they are miles away—far from being actively and cognitively engaged. And unfortunately, too often students choose to respond to the boredom and disengagement by simply dropping out of school entirely. If stand-and-deliver teaching isn't good enough for our professional development seminars, why would it be good enough for our children?

This book aims to provide an alternative to stand-and-deliver teaching through Total Participation Techniques (first introduced in Himmele & Himmele, 2009). We hope to provide ways to actively and cognitively engage all students in the learning process. We have written this book for teachers, using real classroom examples and a variety of field-tested techniques that can be implemented in your classrooms tomorrow. It is also for administrators who want to provide teachers with a toolkit of such techniques and a model for analyzing lessons in a way that can help teachers make their classrooms engaging places where the content is made relevant and deep to students. It can even be used by college professors and professional developers who are tired of relentlessly lecturing. Yes, even with adult students, these techniques can enhance the delivery and understanding of the concepts that you are hoping to teach. Many of the Total Participation Techniques presented can be modified to work regardless of whether you teach 2nd grade or college physics. As you read, we encourage you to pause and think about how you might modify and apply each technique to the specific audience that you teach.

The Second Edition

The first edition of this book was released in 2011. Since then, the book has been the topic of an award-winning DVD, an online course, and a quick reference guide for planning (all available through ASCD). It has been featured in research studies, several university extension courses, hundreds of professional development sessions, and it has been cited in numerous books, studies, articles, online publications, and school and district improvement plans.

We've learned quite a bit more about the power of instruction that is cognitively engaging, and as a result we have included the following:

- 51 TPTs (the first edition had 37), and a new chapter with techniques for "Wrap-Ups"
- New research featuring TPTs and supporting their use
- Updated research for existing topics and research related to student attention and learning
- Emphasis on important components, such as Ripple Questioning
- Common pitfalls that we've noticed as we've observed TPT lessons since the release of the first edition and solutions for avoiding them
- A more extensive Appendix describing Bloom's original and revised taxonomies and Webb's Depth of Knowledge
- An Appendix that contains reminder posters for helping teachers remember to ripple and maximize their use of TPTs

Book Overview

This book covers the *why* and the *how* of Total Participation Techniques (TPTs). First we look at the *why* in Chapters 1 and 2, exploring the heavy toll that disengagement is taking on student success. In the United States, slightly more than 20 percent of students fail to graduate from high school (DePaoli, Balfanz, & Bridgeland, 2016; Rennie Center for Education Research & Policy, 2012). Although most students graduate in spite of disengagement and boredom, they fail to flex their cognitive muscle and develop higher-order thinking skills that could have made the learning deep, lasting, and meaningful. We believe that the use of TPTs could have made a difference for these students. The *how* is addressed in Chapter 3 on tools and supplies, such as TPT toolkits, that allow for smooth and seamless infusions of TPTs in your classrooms. Then, in Chapters 4 through 8, we present the actual techniques for ensuring total participation. Most of the presentations include the following four sections:

Description—We present an overview of the technique.

How It Works—We present specific steps for using the technique.

How to Ensure Higher-Order Thinking—We present ideas for going beyond surface-level comprehension.

Pause to Apply—We encourage teachers to adapt and personalize the technique to the contexts and content areas that they teach.

Chapters 9 and 10 address how TPTs function as formative assessments and how to create "TPT-conducive" classrooms. Finally, in the Afterword, we address common pitfalls with regard to effectively implementing TPTs.

This book is also a visit to modern-day schools, with teachers who created TPT-conducive classrooms. You'll meet the following excellent teachers from Manheim Central Middle School in south-central Pennsylvania:

Meghan Babcock, 6th grade teacher

Matt Baker, 8th grade English teacher

Courtney Cislo, 5th grade teacher

Liz Lubeskie, 8th grade history teacher

Shannon Paules, 7th and 8th grade English teacher

Keely Potter, reading specialist

Mike Pyle, 5th grade teacher

Julie Wash, 6th grade teacher

We included insightful conversations with these teachers, who eloquently phrased what we had hoped to convey to you. At the time of the observations, the teachers ranged in teaching experience from 2 to 16 years, with an average of 9 years. Their implementation of the techniques provides this book with real-life examples of how you might implement the same techniques in your content areas. Several of the teachers now hold different positions than those that were held at the time of our interviews and observations. To avoid confusion, their grade levels and positions appear as they were at the time of our classroom visits.

We also have included examples from Heather Berrier, a 5th grade student teacher from Millersville University. Heather's impressive implementation of TPTs in her daily lessons proves that TPTs can work for novices as well as experienced teachers. In this second edition, several other teachers are featured as well. We hope that this book will spark conversations among teachers and administrators around the topic of active participation and deep cognitive engagement for students. We also hope that you will begin conversations with us. You can contact us via our website, www.TotalParticipationTechniques.com, where you may also find helpful tools and resources, and join the mailing list for updates on content.

Section 1:

TPTs and Engagement

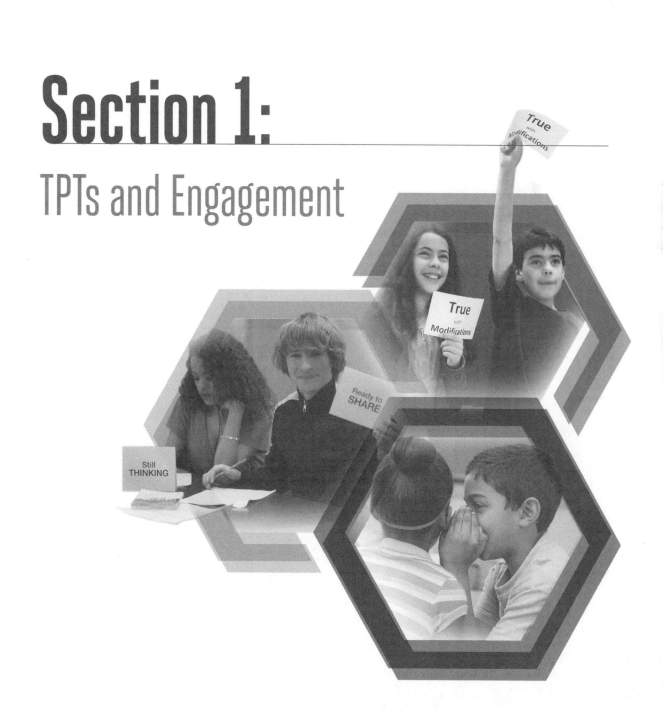

1

The High Cost of Disengagement

Train teachers to call only on students who raise their hands and to build on correct responses to maintain a brisk classroom pace. This would enhance the self-confidence of already proficient students and minimize class participation and engagement among those who enter with lower proficiency.

Kim Marshall, "A How-to Plan for Widening the Gap"

Think about the typical question-and-answer session in most classrooms. We call it "the beach ball scenario" because it reminds us of a scene in which a teacher is holding a beach ball. She tosses it to a student, who quickly catches the ball and tosses it back. She then tosses it to another student. The same scenario happens perhaps three or four times during what is poorly referred to as a "class discussion." Although the teacher asks three or four questions, only two or three eager students actually get an opportunity to demonstrate active cognitive engagement with the topic at hand (we say two or three because a couple of enthusiastic students usually answer more than one question). Often even seasoned teachers can relate to the problem of calling out a question and getting a response from only one or two students. They get little feedback from the others and don't get an accurate assessment of what the others have learned until it's too late. They remember the beach ball scenario because for many, they did it just yesterday. Let's face it: we can all get stuck in the beach ball scenario.

The problem with tossing the beach ball is that too many students sit, either passively or actively disengaged, giving no indication of what they are thinking or of what they have learned. They have effectively learned to fly beneath the radar. Do you remember doing the same thing? Was it a high school or an upper-elementary content class many moons ago? Did you actually even read the book? Well, we'll make no confessions here, for fear that high school diplomas can actually be revoked after issuance. But our point is this: unless you intentionally plan for and require students to demonstrate active participation and cognitive engagement with the topic that you are teaching, *you have no way of knowing what students are learning until it's often too late to repair misunderstandings.* With approximately six hours of actual instructional time per school day, what percentage of that time are students actively engaged and cognitively invested in what is being taught or learned in your classroom? What evidence do we as teachers have that students are actually cognitively in tune with us? And what wonderful and deep critical thinking are we missing out on by not requiring evidence of processing and content-based interactions by our students?

Research on Total Participation Techniques

If we were given the opportunity to choose just one tool that could dramatically improve teaching and learning, we would choose Total Participation Techniques as the quickest, simplest, most effective vehicle for doing so. Whether you're a student teacher, a novice teacher, or even a 30-year veteran, a total-participation mindset is essential for ensuring active participation and cognitive engagement by all of your learners, as well as for providing you with effective ongoing formative assessments. *Total Participation Techniques (TPTs) are teaching techniques that allow for all students to demonstrate, at the same time, active participation and cognitive engagement in the topic being studied.* Quite simply, we believe that if you infuse your teaching with TPTs, you'll be a stronger teacher and fewer students will fall through the cracks of our educational system. TPTs can make us all better teachers.

A study conducted in four North Texas schools, with 211 5th grade English language learners (ELLs), found that those who attended the two TPT-practicing schools outperformed those in the two non-TPT-practicing schools on standardized reading tests. Studies involving comparisons of ELLs are often subject to numerous variables that affect how data might appear. The biggest issue with studies involving ELLs is that of dissimilar proficiency levels of students in the schools being compared. However, when comparing monitored students who had been exited within two years, whose proficiency levels would likely be similar, the students in the TPT-practicing schools outperformed those in the non-TPT-practicing schools at the end of the year on standardized reading tests (de la Isla, 2015).

The importance of student engagement is not limited to K–12 classrooms. University professors Witkowski and Cornell (2015) used the TPT Cognitive Engagement Model (Himmele & Himmele, 2011) and quadrant analyses to investigate the effects of collaborative activities and TPTs on student engagement and learning for 95 students in two undergraduate literacy classes. The results prompted them to make revisions to their courses that supported an increase in the level of cognitive engagement on the part of all students. According to Witkowski and Cornell, "the TPT Cognitive Engagement Model and Quadrant Analysis helped us to dramatically change our methods of teaching" (p. 63). Self-reported student learning and motivation increased as a result of the integration of TPTs and collaborative approaches to teaching as well (Witkowski & Cornell, 2015). The TPT Cognitive Engagement Model will be further described in Chapter 2.

The more we observe excellent teachers teach, the more convinced we become that the common thread in their teaching is ensuring that students become actively, cognitively, and emotionally engaged in the content being taught. And although we are the first to admit that "there is nothing new under the sun" and that the idea behind TPTs is truly a simple concept, we too often see that the actual implementation of techniques that cognitively engage students is not the norm in many classrooms. This situation is true whether we visit urban schools, rural schools, or well-to-do suburban schools. We find over and over again, too many teachers continue to fall back into the same old pattern of "delivering" the content while allowing their students to fall into the pattern of delivering passive stares. Too much focus is often placed on the teacher as the distributor of knowledge. A TPT mindset can effectively take the focus off of teaching and place it on what, and to what extent, your students are learning.

Listening Objects

Unfortunately, as mentioned in the Introduction to this book, too much of today's teaching is characterized by a stand-and-deliver approach to presenting content, in which teachers simply stand at the front of the room and deliver the material to be learned. Paolo Freire (2000) describes students in this type of a scenario as "listening objects" (p. 71). Would you like to be a *listening object*? Think about it. Would it warm your heart to know that daily you pack your children's lunches and they eagerly race off to school, where they sit and become someone's *listening objects*? Education built around the notion of listening objects or stand-and-deliver teaching is not effective for young minds, and it doesn't work for adults either. At any age, people need to pause and process what they're learning. They need to chew on concepts, jot down their thoughts, compare understandings with peers, articulate their questions, and as reading specialist Keely Potter puts it, "celebrate the learning that is happening right now in my head."

Disengaging and Dropping Out

Every nine seconds, a student drops out of school (Lehr, Johnson, Bremer, Cosio, & Thompson, 2004). Although recent indicators point to progress within overall graduation rates, even the encouraging reports still indicate that a fifth of our students drop out (DePaoli et al., 2016; Rennie Center for Education Research & Policy, 2012). The picture is bleakest for African Americans, Latinos, and Native Americans, whose dropout percentages are more than twice that of their white peers (Balfanz, Bridgeland, Moore, & Hornig Fox, 2010). Because much of our experience is with students in urban schools, we have a very real understanding that effective teaching can have a direct influence on a student's life choices.

For six years we both volunteered in California's Chino State Prisons (Bill in the men's, Pérsida in the women's). If you don't yet understand the effect that your teaching can have on students, consider volunteering in a prison. The experience will make you an instant believer in the power of your teaching. In prisons, illiteracy is rampant. Dropping out of high school is not the exception—it is the norm. In fact, three-quarters of state prison inmates are dropouts (Martin & Halperin, 2006). And academic self-confidence is close to nonexistent among prisoners. As soon as inmates discovered we were teachers, many would freely tell us about their academic inadequacies and failures. Many were quick to place the full extent of the blame on themselves.

The cost of school failure doesn't end with the incarcerated. Think about the toll incarceration takes on the children of inmates, including the vicious circle of incarceration. We have both met mothers and fathers whose daughters and sons were serving a prison sentence at the same time as the parents. What kinds of educational experiences did these men and women participate in? Did they become "listening objects"? Would a better education have made a difference?

Boredom and Engagement

The reasons for dropping out vary depending on the students, but among the top reasons—cited by the dropouts themselves—are boredom and the irrelevance of school (America's Promise Alliance, 2014; Bridgeland, DiIulio, & Morison, 2006). For most dropouts, becoming listening objects didn't work. When high school students talked about the types of teaching they wanted, they "described their preferred instructional strategies as ones that were hands-on, and that contained opportunities for debate and discussion" (Certo, Cauley, Moxley, & Chafin, 2008, p. 32). In other words, they preferred engagement, or just the opposite of boredom. These same researchers found that one of the negative consequences of a heavy emphasis on broad curricular coverage aimed at meeting academic standards was that "the quality of instruction is less engaging to students" (p. 26). A 2015 Gallup poll, surveying close to a million students, found that 50 percent of 5th through 12th graders reported being "not engaged" or "actively disengaged" in school. The more students advanced in grade levels, the less likely they were to agree with the statement "In the last seven days, I have learned something interesting at school."

Several studies and high school reform initiatives cite student engagement as a key ingredient in helping students stay in school and be successful (ASCD, 2010; Bridgeland et al., 2006; Lehr et al., 2004; Ream & Rumberger, 2008; Voke, 2002). According to a student respondent in the 2009 High School Survey of Student Engagement, "I think that the teachers have a lot to do with how you feel about school. Some teachers do well in engaging you and others never engage anyone" (Yazzie-Mintz, 2010, p. 20). Though failure to engage students would certainly not be intentional, it may in large part be owed to the prevalence of lesson delivery methods based primarily on lecture. David Sousa (2006) reports 4 to 10 times more retention when students are involved in verbal and visual processing (audiovisual, demonstration, and discussion groups) than when they are exposed to verbal processing alone (lecture and reading). After 24 hours, average students retain an average of 5 percent of what was lectured, 10 percent of what was read, 50 percent of what was learned as a result of being involved in a discussion group, and 90 percent of what they immediately used or taught to others. Teaching others, and immediately using what is learned, results in 19 times the retention as what is learned in lecture format. However, Sousa also states that "despite the impressive amount of evidence about how little students retain from lecture, it continues to be the most prevalent method of teaching, especially in secondary and higher education" (p. 94).

Making a Difference

Why would we, as authors of a book dedicated to infusing your classrooms with fun, interactive, participatory, and cognitively engaging strategies, dwell on something as depressing as the dropout problem? We do so because we know that for some students, cognitively engaging experiences can literally mean the difference between life and death. In case you think we are exaggerating, think about how dropping out is connected to crime and incarceration. Moretti (2005) estimates, through his meta-analysis, that "a one-year increase in average years of schooling reduces murder and assault by almost 30%, motor vehicle theft by 20%, arson by 13%, and burglary and larceny by about 6%" (p. 6). Bridgeland, DiIulio, and Morison (2006) calculate that a dropout is more than eight times as likely to be in jail or prison as a person with at least a high school diploma. The less education that inmates have, the more likely they are to return to prison (Harlow, 2003).

We know that effective teaching makes a difference (Black, 2016; Tucker & Stronge, 2005). In fact, an analysis of student academic growth over time suggests that teacher effectiveness has a greater influence on student performance than race, socioeconomic status, or class size (Darling-Hammond, 2000; Sanders & Horn, 1998). The cumulative residual effects of ineffective teaching last for years, even after exposure to ineffective teaching has been followed by exposure to effective teaching (Jordan, Mendro, & Weerasinghe, 1997; Sanders & Rivers, 1996). In sum, the quality of education a child receives is highly dependent on the effectiveness of that child's teachers.

Whether you work in suburban or urban schools, teaching average performers, gifted high achievers and underachievers, children of immigrants, students with special needs, students who repeatedly experience school failure, or simply your average passive performer teetering between staying in and dropping out, your excellence in effective teaching could be the answer to parents' prayers and the vehicle by which they see their dreams for their son or daughter realized. One teacher can make such a difference.

Evidence of Active Participation

In 2014, a blog post by Alexis Wiggins, 15-year teaching veteran and daughter of the late education guru Grant Wiggins, went viral. It was picked up by several major news outlets, including Valerie Strauss's column in the *Washington Post*. Wiggins had spent two days shadowing two students before she took on a new role as a high school learning coach.

These were her key takeaways (Wiggins, in Strauss, 2014):

- Key Takeaway #1: Students sit all day, and sitting is exhausting.
- Key Takeaway #2: High school students are sitting passively and listening during approximately 90 percent of their classes.
- Key Takeaway #3: Students feel a little bit like a nuisance all day long. ("I lost count of how many times we were told to be quiet and pay attention.")

Wiggins's discoveries are so important to the process of becoming an effective teacher that we've made her blog post required reading for our student teacher candidates. It contains essential reminders that we all need to hear periodically that can help to place us in the shoes of our students.

The use of Total Participation Techniques provides teachers with evidence of active participation and cognitive engagement. They can have a direct effect on the reasons most students drop out or fail to meet their academic potential. For one thing, in a TPT-conducive classroom, students are not allowed to be passive and hide behind the others who are always raising their hands. All students are demonstrating that they are learning and interacting and—believe it or not—doing so while they're having a great time. You will notice that all the techniques we present require active processing at deep levels of thinking, and all but a few use interaction.

Manheim Central Middle School

Let's look at the socially tenuous and risk-conscious environment that is often present in a typical middle school classroom. According to Keely Potter, a reading specialist at Manheim Central Middle School in south-central Pennsylvania, "By the time many students hit middle school, disengagement has become a learned behavior—not for all, but for some, especially those that hold little social capital among their peers. Too many are either resistant to engagement, afraid to engage, or afraid to appear *too* engaged. So that's one of the most important things that we can try to undo as effective middle school teachers."

Keely and several other teachers at the middle school made it their priority to infuse TPTs into their daily curriculum. They graciously invited us into their classrooms and are the source of many of the examples we use throughout this book. The best teaching that we have observed involves teachers setting the stage for students to demonstrate cognitive engagement in activities that require time to process, to make connections, and to interact with peers as well as their teachers. We are convinced that the accountability and cognitive engagement that result from TPTs can make a difference between mediocrity and excellence in teaching—and between student failure and student success.

When asked about the role of Total Participation Techniques in teaching, 8th grade English teacher Matt Baker said, "I've completely bought into it." He went on to talk about how he arrived at this acceptance. And he shared his thoughts about his earlier eight years of teaching experience in a high school:

> Student interaction was rare. The idea of kids sharing something with one another, and the idea of kids sitting next to one another, was a foreign concept. The mentality was, you can't ever let them work in groups because then one person does all the work and everybody gets a good grade, and it's not fair. Everybody was in rows; if they were sharing something, it meant they were cheating. But that type of teaching doesn't work. Kids need to talk to one another. They cannot sit in a classroom for a whole period and not process what they are learning with one another.

In contrast, Baker's classroom at Manheim Central Middle School was characterized by a consistent give-and-take among students, and among students and the teacher. Students were constantly stopping, pairing up, and then joining other pairs to form small groups in order to process meaningful and complex concepts being presented through articles and literary works that were relevant to their own lives. Even if students wanted to sleep in Baker's class, they wouldn't be able to. Once a brief reading or content presentation had ended, students were out of their seats demonstrating that they could connect these concepts to their lives and to the effect that these issues have on society. In Baker's classroom, standards were met under the cover of relevance. And students were anxious to share their own take on the issues presented.

Ease of Use

It is not difficult to cognitively engage students, and it doesn't take much work. Sixth grade teacher Meghan Babcock and reading specialist Keely Potter implemented a four-week TPT-infused unit using Kate DiCamillo's book *The Tiger Rising* (2001). According to Babcock,

> Using TPTs, the students were right with us every step of the way. It wasn't a lot of work; it just streamlined my thinking. It put more structures in place. I did the same amount of planning; I just did it in a little bit of a different way . . . even just taking the questions out of the curriculum [or standards] and doing your own little thing makes a huge difference.

According to two-year veteran Courtney Cislo, implementing TPTs is not dependent on the amount of experience a teacher has. All teachers can improve their teaching through TPT-infused lessons:

> I think for teachers that have never taught before, these techniques are so valuable, because you come out of college thinking, "OK, I'm going to do this as my anticipatory set, and then I'll do this, and next I'll read that, and finally I'll close with this." It's all me, me, me, and I, I, I. But the point is not to get your own agenda across; the point is that the students learn. With these techniques, you can gauge, "Oh, they've got it and I can move on," or "I should move more quickly," or "Uh-oh, I need to go back and reteach." It's a critical element for any classroom no matter how much experience a teacher has.

Although implementing TPTs may require that you actively remind yourself to do so, if you stick to it, it becomes a way of thinking. Babcock found that "the more you deliberately implement them, the more they become an expectation." Fifth grade teacher Mike Pyle agrees: "I use them every day throughout every lesson. The more you use them, the more comfortable you become with using them." But he also points out that intentionality is required:

You really have to be intentional in the beginning of the year, because many students are used to traditional classrooms where they sit in rows. But for me, I have to have them in groups. They have to be sitting in clusters, because they do so much discussing of things back and forth, with face partners, shoulder buddies, and as a whole group as well. We do a lot of sharing. For example, in social studies, even when they are reading out of the text, I might have them read a section, and then they have to stop and relay what they learned to their teammates. This back-and-forth helps them remember what they learned.

TPTs work best in classrooms that practice this constant back-and-forth, from the text or teachers to students, from students to students, and from students to teachers. By definition, TPTs require active participation and cognitive engagement by everyone.

Additional Thoughts

Before we move on, we need to make a disclaimer. We are still developing in our own use of TPTs. In many instances we have discovered the importance of TPTs the hard way. And we still have days in our university classes when we simply talk too much. We've come to realize that when we are engaged and passionate about a topic, it's easy to get lost in our own talking—even when no one is listening. The wheels in our minds are turning, and the generation of ideas is refreshing (to us) as we talk and talk and talk, and everyone else is thinking about the many things on their to-do lists. One student is focusing on the phone call she just received, another on the laundry he forgot to take out of the washer three days ago, and yet another on life's important questions, like whether or not that mole on her arm is starting to look like her Aunt Martha. This is why we no longer rely on our own good judgment to inject TPTs in our lessons. We have realized that we need safeguards to ensure against getting lost in the talking. So we now write TPTs into our slides, and we type them into our lesson plan agendas in red so that we don't forget to stop talking. And you just may have to do the same thing in whatever way will help you remember to repeatedly pause for student processing, interaction, and the reciprocity that needs to take place between students and students, as well as between teachers and students. Appendix B contains reminder posters that you can display in your classroom with the goal of helping you remember to use TPTs as often as you can.

Deep cognitive engagement does not emerge from simply being *talked at.* "Knowledge emerges only through invention and re-invention, through the restless, impatient, continuing, hopeful inquiry human beings pursue in the world, with the world, and with each other" (Freire, 2000, p. 72). We have the ability to make this restless, impatient, continuing, and hopeful inquiry happen in our classrooms. But it will take a deliberate infusion of opportunities to process, reflect, question, and interact with each other. So this is what we aim to do in this text: to provide teachers with simple activities that make it difficult for students to think about the phone call, the laundry, or that mole. Instead, students will be too busy actively processing deep concepts in ways that require that they use higher-order thinking as they actively reflect on, analyze, and defend their judgments in meaningful interactions with their peers.

One student who participated in Potter and Babcock's TPT-infused unit offered this reflection: "I have family problems, and when I come here, it all seems perfect, and it goes away." This is our hope—that through the use of TPTs, students will become so actively engaged and so lost in the learning, they won't have time to be distracted by other things.

Reflection Questions

- During your last lesson(s), how much responsibility for demonstrating cognitive engagement did you place on your students?
- Which of your students would most benefit from your consistent use of TPTs?
- How can implementing Total Participation Techniques make you a better teacher?

2

A Model for Total Participation and Higher-Order Thinking

The TPT Cognitive Engagement Model and Quadrant Analysis helped us to dramatically change our methods of teaching. Previously we had attempted activities that we thought would engage our students during class. . . . Analysis of these activities made us realize that our activities were more in quadrants one and two than in three and four.

P. Witkowski and T. Cornell

In this chapter, we will focus on two tools you can use to plan for cognitively engaging teaching. The first, the TPT Cognitive Engagement Model, will present a way to assess the quality of the teaching and learning that is happening within classrooms. The second, The Ripple, provides a way to visualize approaches toward posing deep prompts and questions in a way that cognitively engages every student.

Consider the effort your brain requires to respond to the following task: *Define human rights.* For most people this task requires that they simply dig into their mental files, find an adequate definition, and complete the task by articulating the definition. Adequately responding to this task does not require a deep analysis of the concept and what the concept entails. On Bloom's cognitive taxonomy, it would be considered a lower-order question.

Now consider the effort your brain would require to answer this question: *How has your perception of human rights been affected by your culture and your country's history?* To successfully answer this question, you have to dig quite a bit further. You have to locate cognitive files on what you know about human rights, your culture's perceptions of human rights, how people's perceptions of human rights have changed over time, how other cultures view human rights, and how your perceptions might have differed if you had been born in a different culture or before certain historic events in your own country. Answering the question requires analyzing, making connections, drawing conclusions, and basing those conclusions on what you know about historic events and the resulting societal changes. On Bloom's cognitive taxonomy, this would be considered a higher-order question. It requires that you flex your cognitive muscle, and make numerous cognitive connections between what you've learned and what you already know.

Creating classroom opportunities for developing higher-order thinking is essential for helping students become the critical thinkers, problem solvers, innovators, and change makers upon which every society thrives. In writing this book, we wanted to be careful to make sure that TPTs were not simply used as another way of getting one-word answers or answers that would be considered superficial knowledge from students. With all of the TPTs, we need to aim for deeper learning, because a teacher can use an activity that ensures total participation but still perpetuate the lower-order thinking that might have been present in a traditional question-and-answer session. Except for the fact that all students are answering, a teacher could implement TPTs ineffectively and only require that students regurgitate forgettable facts. Our goal is to move students beyond shallow and superficial understandings and toward learning that is cognitively intense, meaningful, and deep. Note that Bloom's cognitive taxonomy, lower- and higher-order thinking, and Webb's Depth of Knowledge are further explained in Appendix A.

Ensuring Higher-Order Thinking

The use of prompts that require higher-order thinking is what takes students beyond simple engagement. It ensures that students are *cognitively* engaged. Students aren't just engaged and having fun; they are also thinking deeply. The need to emphasize higher-order thinking is why we felt compelled to include sections on "How to Ensure Higher-Order Thinking" for most of the techniques presented. Student interaction will only be as powerful as your prompts. So take the time to develop prompts and activities that require students to reflect and analyze, evaluate, and synthesize their learning. Be sure that you provide opportunities for students to explore the big picture in lessons and justify responses based on concepts learned.

Done well, TPTs can require that students make connections from the classroom content to real life. This process works best when teachers have thought through the big picture of their lessons and understand what is most important for students to walk away with. Your students will not remember everything you try to teach them, just the meaningful parts, so focus on deep meaning. In this way, relevance will be made transparent to your students. What is the big picture in your content objectives? How can you make it relevant? Through the act of ensuring higher-order thinking, you engage children in thinking through the implications and the relevance of the content to their world. They are looking intently within the nuances of the conceptual understandings so as to be lost in connection making. Like the student quoted at the end of Chapter 1, whose problems seem to go away when she comes to class, we want children to get "lost" in the learning.

The TPT Cognitive Engagement Model

The TPT Cognitive Engagement Model (see Figure 2.1) is aimed at helping you visualize the relationship between total participation and higher-order thinking in your classroom. Evidence of learning will occur when students are actively participating and developing higher-order thinking, as is the case when activities fit into Quadrant 4 in the model. Although all of the quadrants may reflect important aspects of your teaching, be sure to shift back to Quadrant 4 throughout your lesson to allow students to process and interact regarding the learning.

To help you get a feel for how this type of teaching might look in a real-life classroom, Figure 2.1 includes an analysis of a lesson taught by 5th grade teacher Courtney Cislo. In the figure, we analyze her teaching in terms of the quadrants to provide you with an example of how shifting among quadrants, with a predominance in Quadrant 4, can provide more cognitively engaging learning experiences for students.

Teaching that gets stuck in Quadrant 1 (Low Cognition/Low Participation) is problematic for several reasons. What evidence is there that students are processing what was taught? Because the content is using lower-order thinking, how important is it and how long will it stick? Are students perceiving this content as relevant? What is going on in their minds as they sit and pretend to listen to the teacher?

Figure 2.1

TPT Cognitive Engagement Model and Quadrant Analysis

Quadrant	Sequence of Activities in Courtney Cislo's Lesson on Judgments
3	2:38–2:40 Cislo read a moral dilemma (a story with a moral conflict).
4	2:40–2:45 Cislo asked students to respond to the first moral dilemma by grabbing the card that best matched their emotions. "How do you feel about how the problem was solved? Be ready to explain why you feel this way." Students took out their Appointment Agendas, found their 2:00 appointment, and shared the emotion card they chose and the reason behind it.
4	2:45–2:47 Cislo stopped the students and asked the pairs to go one step further by sharing with each other why they believed what they believed. "What personal values or experiences are affecting your judgment of this scenario?"
3	2:47–2:50 All students were seated again. Cislo read a second moral dilemma.
4	2:50–2:53 Cislo asked students to choose an emotion card and repeat the 2:40–2:45 process, this time with their 5:00 appointment. "This time discuss how you feel, why you feel that way, and your personal values or experiences that cause you to feel this way." She referred to the flow chart and to the directions written on the board as she spoke.
3	2:53–2:55 Cislo read a third moral dilemma involving Miley Cyrus (the students demonstrated strong opinions about this topic).
4	2:55–2:57 Students were asked to select an emotion card and share in pairs at their tables (due to time constraints).
4	2:57–2:59 In a Quick-Write, students were asked to "define the word *judgment* and explain why your judgments were not the same as those of your classmates."

continued

Figure 2.1 (*continued*)

TPT Cognitive Engagement Model and Quadrant Analysis

Quadrant	Sequence of Activities in Courtney Cislo's Lesson on Judgments
4	2:59–3:01 Students were asked to pair-share their Quick-Writes at their tables.
3	3:01–3:03 Volunteers were selected to share with class.
3	3:03–3:04 Cislo summarized a final definition for judgments as she again referred to the flowchart. Quick-Writes were collected.

Cislo's lesson provided a nice blend of content presentation and student responsibility. She continuously asked students to demonstrate, through the use of Total Participation Techniques, that they were actively processing the concepts using higher-order thinking. She circulated and commented on key words as students interacted.

Note: The final Quick-Writes would make a great source of student-authored material that can be used on a One-Liner Wall (see Chapter 9) for revisiting the themes in the lesson.

Source: From *Total Participation Techniques: Making Every Student an Active Learner*, 1st ed. (pp. 15–16), by P. Himmele and W. Himmele, 2011, Alexandria, VA: ASCD. Copyright © 2011 by ASCD. Adapted with permission.

Teaching that lingers in Quadrant 2 (Low Cognition/High Participation) allows students to review and often apply what they have learned, but frequently what they have learned is easily forgotten because it is not linked to anything deep. Because it required high participation, it may have been fun; but because it required only lower-order thinking, it also was very forgettable.

Teaching that lingers in Quadrant 3 (High Cognition/Low Participation) may be an improvement from Quadrant 1, but for whom? Teaching that is predominantly represented in Quadrant 3 is selective in requiring evidence of higher-order thinking only from certain students. An article titled "The 'Receivement Gap'" (Chambers, 2009) addresses the inequity in access to high-quality educational opportunities. Chambers argues that the achievement gap is largely due to unequal access to high-quality learning experiences for students tracked into classrooms with fewer learning opportunities. We believe that a *receivement gap* also exists within classrooms when we operate predominantly in Quadrant 3. The students who always participate and have their hands up are the ones who benefit from the higher-order questions prepared by the teacher. If your lessons tend to linger in Quadrant 3, TPTs can ensure that all of your students are benefiting from the higher-order thinking that currently only a few are experiencing.

It is important that we structure our teaching so that every lesson includes several opportunities for all students to demonstrate active participation and cognitive engagement in what we are teaching. Activities in Quadrant 4 (High Cognition/High Participation) allow us to obtain evidence of this. Although there will be times when we want to make sure students comprehend basic understandings necessary to get them to higher-order thinking, our ultimate goal is that students be able to analyze, evaluate, and synthesize what they've learned. This goal is what keeps us moving back to Quadrant 4 periodically throughout our lessons.

Consider using the quadrants in Figure 2.1 to analyze your planning. As you work with teams or instructional coaches, consider asking a peer to observe you. In which quadrants did you tend to linger? Could a question have been better posed through a TPT to ensure that all students benefited rather than just a select few?

We encourage you to use the TPT Cognitive Engagement Model to analyze your own planning, as well as to help you support your colleagues in their teaching. If you are an administrator, the model can also help you in supporting your teachers in their planning or as you analyze lessons that you observe. A reminder poster containing an image of the Cognitive Engagement Model quadrants is included in Appendix B. Additional resources and a professional development activity can be found on our website at www.TotalParticipationTechniques.com.

The Ripple

In Chapter 1, we described what we called "the beach ball" scenario, where a teacher poses a question to the whole class and calls on a handful of volunteers who choose to respond. One of the consequences of the beach ball scenario is that after a teacher has gone through the trouble of creating great prompts aimed at higher-order thinking, only a handful of students get to demonstrate that they have processed the question. To ensure that all students are reflecting on and responding to the prompt, we encourage teachers to "ripple" their questions (Himmele & Himmele, 2009). Rather than using the traditional question-and-answer approach where a teacher poses a question to the class as a whole, rippling begins with every student responding (individually) to a prompt, then sharing that response in pairs or small groups, followed by volunteers sharing with the class. We call this a ripple because it starts with the entry of a pebble into water—also known as your question or prompt—to which every student individually responds. The next ripples move outward from the student's individual response into pairs or small groups, and finally the ripples reach the whole group.

In most traditional question-and-answer sessions, teachers skip the individual reflection time, which would allow for deeper learning on the part of every individual student. Instead of starting with the whole group, keep every student accountable for learning by structuring your prompts so that every student is given an opportunity to *individually* reflect on and react to the prompt. This can be by way of Quick-Writes, Quick-Draws, or other techniques suggested in Chapters 4 through 8. This individual reflection time is important for all students, even if it's only two minutes long. Then the ripple moves outward when you ask students to join up with a peer (see Figure 2.2) and share and interact regarding their responses to the prompt. The outer ripple appears as you ask pairs to join existing pairs, or as you open up the floor to the larger class, eliciting responses once students have had time to bounce ideas off each other. Now that students have shared and met with success with their peers, they will be more likely to respond in a larger group. One thing is certain: students are not likely to respond with the dreaded "I don't know" after you've given them the opportunity to reflect individually and then in small groups. By rippling your questions and prompts, you ensure that all of your students are reflecting on prompts aimed at higher-order thinking.

Allowing students time to individually collect and record their thoughts, and then rippling outward with Pair-Shares or small groups before bringing them to the whole class, provides students the security of having already met with success. Sixth grader Ariel shared her appreciation for the way Quick-Writes and Pair-Shares were implemented using this ripple approach: "I liked it because you get to share your feelings with one person instead of saying them in front of the whole class." Socially tentative students are not the only ones who will benefit; students with certain special needs and English language learners will especially benefit from using the Ripple, which gives them time to process their own thinking individually and then in pairs or small groups, laying the groundwork for them to feel comfortable enough to share their thoughts with the class.

When reading student reflections regarding her unit on imagery, metaphors, and symbolism, Keely Potter noted that "some of the big trends that students touched on, the comfortable and safe environment, was what I

Figure 2.2
The Ripple

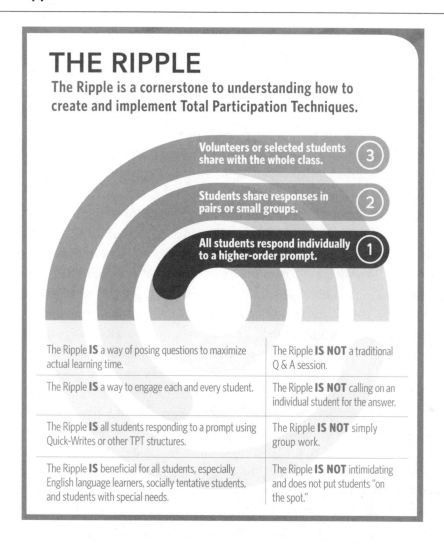

THE RIPPLE
The Ripple is a cornerstone to understanding how to create and implement Total Participation Techniques.

3 — Volunteers or selected students share with the whole class.

2 — Students share responses in pairs or small groups.

1 — All students respond individually to a higher-order prompt.

The Ripple **IS** a way of posing questions to maximize actual learning time.	The Ripple **IS NOT** a traditional Q & A session.
The Ripple **IS** a way to engage each and every student.	The Ripple **IS NOT** calling on an individual student for the answer.
The Ripple **IS** all students responding to a prompt using Quick-Writes or other TPT structures.	The Ripple **IS NOT** simply group work.
The Ripple **IS** beneficial for all students, especially English language learners, socially tentative students, and students with special needs.	The Ripple **IS NOT** intimidating and does not put students "on the spot."

noticed from the get-go." Meghan Babcock agreed and said, "And that was because of our structures and our protocols that ensured that all students have a voice in a nonintrusive way—the Quick-Writes, the Pair-Shares, the Chalkboard Splashes. . . . The safety and the community came so much from these little structures of total participation being built in." A reminder poster aimed at helping you remember to ripple is included in Appendix B.

The Problem with Group Brainstorming

The concept of the Ripple begins with each student individually responding to a prompt (aka the initial plunk of a pebble). It can be tempting to start by skipping the first step and instead asking students to simply get into groups to work out the solution to a higher-order prompt. This is often due to the belief that group brainstorming provides a scaffold for students, rather than expecting that students be able to individually tackle higher-order prompts. After all, if one student's thoughts are helpful, then four students' thoughts must be at least four times as helpful, right? However, despite its widespread acceptance, the effectiveness of group brainstorming is not supported by research.

Research tells us that free-flowing group brainstorming can actually stifle creativity. When students are working in groups, each idea that is posed ends up setting a course for similar ideas to be pursued, and inhibits the ability for individual group members to entertain dissimilar, or even better, ideas. According to Jonah Lehrer (2012), the term *brainstorming* originated from a chapter in a 1948 surprise best-selling book by Alex Osborn entitled *Your Creative Power.* In Osborn's book, a brainstorm was described as making use of many people attacking a problem. Though the idea took off and is still used in businesses, boardrooms, and classrooms, Lehrer's review of the literature on group brainstorming points to evidence that it actually does not work. According to research psychologist Keith Sawyer, "Decades of research have consistently shown that brainstorming groups think of far fewer ideas than the same number of people who work alone and later pool their ideas" (cited in Lehrer, 2012). In terms of quality, brainstorming doesn't work, either. Studies actually show that students working alone and then pooling their ideas is a much more effective and efficient use of a group's brainpower. Not only are there more ideas, but the ideas are also deemed to be of higher quality.

Calling on Someone Should Be the Last Thing You Do

We've often heard it said that there is safety in numbers. However, where classroom interactions are concerned, each student should first bring something of value to the group. In fact, when it comes to higher-order questions, calling on someone is fine. In sequence, however, it should be the last thing you do. Wait until every student has processed and responded to your higher-order prompts before posing your prompts in a whole-group setting. Not only does this help keep each student accountable for processing the higher-order prompts, but it also enriches the groups' experiences by increasing the diversity of ideas presented and the quality of the groups' refinements of those ideas.

Whenever you notice that you are using a phrase like "Who can tell me . . . ?" or "Does anyone know . . . ?" stop, and ask yourself if there is a better way, particularly if your question is an important one (see Figure 2.3). In terms of rippling higher-order prompts, calling on someone is fine, but sequentially, it should be the last thing that you do. A reminder poster of Figure 2.3 is included in Appendix B. Let it cause you to pause whenever you're tempted to start off with a traditional Q&A.

Figure 2.3
Reminder of What Not to Ask!

How Long Can Students Pay Attention?

Most likely you've heard the common notion that the typical student's attention span is about 10 to 15 minutes long. That is a well-accepted assumption, but research has called that belief into question. Bunce, Flens, and Neiles (2010) looked at 186 college students' self-reported levels of attention in college chemistry classes. Using electronic clickers, students indicated their attention lapses, along with the perceived duration of the lapses. Surprisingly, the researchers found that attention lapses occur several times within a 10- to 15-minute span, for brief periods of time (1 minute or less), even as early as a "settling in" period that takes place about 30 seconds into the lesson, followed by another attention lapse about 4 or 5 minutes into the lesson. Their study did not support the common notion that attention lapses occur every 10 to 15 minutes. Wilson and Korn's (2007) review of the literature on student attention also found no basis for the assertion that a typical student's attention span is from 10 to 15 minutes. Like Bunce, Flens, and Neiles, they found a great degree of variability with regard to attention. In fact, lapses in student attention likely occur more randomly and more often than conventional beliefs suggest. The implications are important. We can't assume that students walk away with the same knowledge, even if they were exposed to the same content. Random lapses in attention require the need for constant checks for understanding, so that gaps in students' understanding can be addressed.

Not surprisingly, Bunce, Flens, and Neiles found that students' attention was more likely to wander during less interactive activities, such as lecturing. The longer the lecture, the more lapses in attention occurred. "As many predict, student attention is higher during non-lecture pedagogies such as demonstrations and clicker questions" (p. 1442). Student attention also seemed to be reawakened to the content of the subsequent lecture after a nonlecture method was used. "Students report significantly lower attention lapses during lecture segments immediately following a demonstration or clicker question than they did in comparable length lecture segments prior to the use of these pedagogies" (p. 1442). This leads us to believe that *the use of interactive nonlecture pedagogies, such as TPTs, can capture student attention and keep student attention even when the TPT is followed by brief periods of lecture.* This is an important concept that can help us create more engaging lessons. Lecture segments should be sandwiched in between moments of accountability and interaction.

Though Bunce, Flens, and Neiles's study was conducted with college students, the implications of their findings have far-reaching implications for K–12 education. If students in college have numerous attention lapses that cast serious doubt on the overestimation of typical attention spans lasting 10 to 15 minutes, we can expect that the attention lapses of children and adolescents will be similar or even more frequent. Anyone who has spent time with children and adolescents knows that it is unreasonable to assume that they have longer attention spans than college students. In light of the participants, the findings of this study hold even greater significance when teaching children. They suggest that teachers should "strive to improve student attention by using student-centered pedagogies at different times throughout the lecture, not only to decrease student attention lapses but also to increase student attention during the lectures that follow the use of such pedagogies" (p. 1442). Something as simple as having students complete a Quick-Write can cause them to refocus, analyze, and synthesize their learning, as well as engage students for the follow-up directed teaching. Additionally, in our experiences, students are aware of which teachers will be requiring evidence of engagement during the lesson. An 8th grade student we interviewed explained her need for accountability when she told us, "I drift off a lot. Like, one of the classes I go to I call 'my daydreaming class.' When I go in there, I daydream. But in Ms. Keely's class you can't daydream, because if you do, you're gonna miss something important, and at the end of class she asks you to write about what we went over in class, so if you were daydreaming, she'll know you weren't paying attention. So that helps" (Himmele, Himmele, & Potter, 2014, p. 99).

When Students Shine

It is probable that one of the greatest benefits of TPT-infused lessons focused on higher-order thinking is that the students whom you would not expect to shine will start shining right alongside the rest of their peers. Meghan Babcock noticed this in her TPT-infused unit:

> It's been neat to see, because the students in learning support [with mild disabilities] will usually wait for all of the other kids to talk. And through using TPTs, I can see what they're thinking, through their Quick-Writes and just knowing that they have a thought, through Thumbs-Up When Ready. (See TPTs in Chapter 4.)

Keely Potter and Meghan Babcock's reading class began as a mandatory class for some students during the last month of school. But because of a mix-up in scheduling, the final week become voluntary. Potter and Babcock made arrangements with other teachers to take students who chose to complete the unit. We expressed surprise that two-thirds of the students continued to come to the reading class, even though it had been made voluntary and the final school year wrap-ups and celebrations were occurring at the same time in their homerooms. When the students were asked why they volunteered to come to the reading class, here's what a few of them wrote:

- "Because it's fun, and it really helps me think deeper."
- "I loved how you had to figure stuff out [in the book] without it being a mystery."
- "Because I wanted to keep reading and find out what happened. For me, that is something I don't do, but I did!"
- "I wanted to finish the book! And I really loved this class. It was so much fun, and it showed me how to connect and learn more about books."
- "I feel comfortable with this group. Also, I want to keep learning about how to dig deeper so I enjoy books more."

In the student surveys, students expressed a clear note of pride in realizing how they were developing in their own ability to dig deeper. This "digging deeper" was facilitated through the use of TPTs that were created to specifically ensure higher-order thinking. Several students even surprised themselves, as was the case for the student who said, "That is something I don't do, but I did!" Another student wrote, "I never really liked to read, and I got really interested in this book." Let us just clarify: Kate DiCamillo's (2001) book *The Tiger Rising* is an emotionally deep book that explores the complex nature of the relationship between two troubled adolescents. We mention this because the students were not reading an action-packed thriller that starts fast and would have kept them on the edge of their seats. Instead, they were kept engaged through the active processing of the deeper meanings embedded throughout this rich piece of literature, through interactive prompts that engaged higher-order thinking.

What Happens When You Ensure Higher-Order Thinking

The best thing about ensuring higher-order thinking is that students come up with things you would have never expected. As noted in the opening quote for this chapter, students will surprise you because collectively their experiences are broader than yours, and broader than any one individual student's. Higher-order thinking thrives on interaction. When students bounce ideas off each other, the exchange generates more ideas in a nonthreatening setting. Each individual student's ideas start to grow, and the effect is like placing a microphone in front of an amplifier. The thoughts go back and forth, growing in intensity. This effect was noticed by 6th grader Anna, who wrote, "By hearing others' ideas, it gave me some new ideas like, 'Wow, I didn't think of that.' And then I would add more to it." Not only will students surprise you, but they will often even end up surprising themselves. The following quote from another 6th grader, Hannah, illustrates the point:

> I have noticed that I am symbolic in my art and can think deep into what I read because of this [reading] class. . . . Quick-Writes and Pair-Sharing helped me get deeper in the story and let me share what I have to say.

Ensuring higher-order thinking also builds academic confidence. Meghan Babcock offered this example:

> Two students just came and gave me a big hug and said that they couldn't wait for the next class because [reading time] made them feel really smart. They said that they felt like they were really thinking. By saying to me that it makes them feel smart, it's because they feel that they have the opportunity to share what they know. They've come so far, because before these students were really afraid to participate.

How TPTs Were Used to Teach Abstract Thinking

One of the language arts standards that Potter and Babcock chose to focus on during their reading lessons was that of reading, analyzing, and interpreting symbolism, metaphors, and imagery in literature. *The Tiger Rising* (DiCamillo, 2001) provided an excellent literary resource for meeting this standard. Potter and Babcock implemented Total Participation Techniques to engage all students in the process of abstract thinking and meaning making. Here's how they did it.

They began by introducing the concept of symbolism and how authors use it to create feelings. They decided to focus on DiCamillo's use of three major elements: the use of color to create moods; the use of "not-words" to understand the way the main character suppressed emotions (for example, "not-thoughts," "non-song," and "not-crier"); and the use of the "suitcase" to represent the character's denial—as in "He made all his feelings go inside the suitcase; he stuffed them in tight and then sat on the suitcase and locked it shut" (p. 3).

To understand the use of color, Potter and Babcock conducted a Chart-Paper Splash (see Chalkboard Splash in Chapter 4) using large pieces of colored butcher paper. Students silently circulated around the room, markers in hand, and wrote on the colored chart papers how each of the colors made them feel. For example, on the red chart paper students wrote these words, among others: *the path to anger, rage and madness, hot, terrified, evil, devil, upset, Armageddon, embarrassment, fire, angry, mean, love.* The yellow chart paper had words such as *bright, playful, sunny, cheerful, ready to run, the opposite of the saddest moments, life, happy, brightness, flip-flops, sun, brought up from darkness.* Potter noted the rich discussion that followed:

> Bram shared that deep blue is his favorite color, and that started a discussion of how deep blue reminded another of sadness. Students started talking about the deeper concepts that are affected by their own personal interpretation of colors. They brought up spiritual connections like good, evil, heaven, and hell, all in an attempt to try to figure out why the author chose the colors she chose.

Potter and Babcock also introduced a painting to expand on the theme of colors. They analyzed how the artist conveyed a mood and a message through his use of colors. Through the use of prompts, they introduced parallels between artists and authors, noting how the former convey thoughts through pictorial images and the latter through mental imagery.

This is how students were introduced to the symbolism of colors within the text. Then whenever colors were mentioned in the book, students were asked to pause and record their thoughts regarding why the author might have used that color to describe the event (see Figure 2.4). Sixth grader Sara noted, "I love that you can get inside a character's head and you can know that you have to work hard if you want to figure out what something means, instead of [the book] just giving it away." Bram shared his own growing understandings when he wrote, "I noticed that I am understanding the words (feel what the author says) better." And Ariel wrote, "The book is very deep and emotional. I feel that I am being put in Rob's shoes, because it is very detailed and it's very easy to picture his life." Another student said, "This is the first book I have ever really loved."

Students were asked to personalize the concepts of the not-words and the suitcase. As a result, symbolic interpretations started showing up in their writings. For example, Conrad reflected on the relationship between the two

Figure 2.4
Anna's Mood and Color Analysis

Name _Anna_

How does the color affect the mood? How do you feel when you see the picture?

- The Tree's on the left look like a firey burst of color seeking to find life in this city. - And the tree's on the right are as calm as the winter breeze. - The people walking in the center are feeling both of ~~these~~ thoughts for the perfect mood. For the perfect walk. For a

(Reread the last paragraph in Chapter Three) perfect time.

Why does Rob see so much gray outside? Think back to the emotions we associated with colors. What do you think the author's purpose is in using so much gray?

The writer use's so much gray because she wants to emphais that Sistine maybe Rob's light he see's gray right now but when Sistine captures Rob's heart his life will not be like this anymore his life will change and the tiger started it all. With him seeing the bright orange tiger. And his heart starting to glow.

☺ Go Anna!

main characters in this way: "Sistine is like a mirror to him. He can talk to her like she's him." After being shown an image of Michelangelo's Sistine Chapel, students were asked to reflect on why the author might have chosen to use the Sistine Chapel as imagery in her book. Ariel wrote, "It represents his life and feelings. When God and Adam are reaching out to one another, it reminds him of his mom reaching out to him."

Quick-Writes, Quick-Draws, Pair-Shares, Networking, Ranking, Cut-and-Pastes, Chalkboard Splashes, Graphic Organizers, Key-Word Dances, Thumbs-Up When Ready, and Bounce Cards were all used as ways for students to process and share their thoughts regarding the prompts (see Chapters 4 through 7 for descriptions of these TPTs). Babcock noted the following: "We did a TPT with each of the activities, and they carried these through. Because we did the TPTs together at the same time, we didn't have to review a whole lot, because you know you've all done the same thinking."

When asked about the importance of understanding the deeper purposes behind the specific items found within state standards, Potter explained it this way:

> Symbolism certainly can be taught as an isolated skill for the purposes of test-taking. But what's missing is the context, the experience, all the *connect-the-dot* points that allow students to go much deeper into symbolism and notice the language that is being used. "What does this word mean?" "How is the author using it?" It could be so easily enhanced with Total Participation Techniques. So many teachers take it to that point of skill mastery. But if a student is a masterful worksheet writer, but they get to the point that when they need to talk about symbolism and do something with it, they first need to look it up in the dictionary and write it down, then we've missed the point and purpose for why students need to know this. You can't just deliver this stuff. It has to be experienced.

Potter and Babcock guided students to experience the reading, analysis, and interpretation of symbolism, metaphors, and imagery through carefully structured TPT-infused lessons that provided students with opportunities for reflection and interaction. In Babcock's words, "Doing activities like this teaches kids *how* to think, not *what* to think."

When teachers carefully structure the delivery of their content so as to ensure active participation and cognitive engagement by every learner, they help ensure that the learning will be lasting and meaningful. And they ensure that not one student will be abandoned along the way. In Chapters 4 through 8, we introduce specific Total Participation Techniques. Most have suggestions on how to use them in ways to ensure higher-order thinking in each learner. As you examine the techniques, think about how you might use, or adapt, each one within your content area.

Reflection Questions

- What units will you be teaching over the next few weeks? How might you ripple your prompts and infuse your lessons with TPTs that help students think through the concepts using higher-order thinking and total participation?
- How might TPTs have helped you during your academic journey, either in your K–12 schooling or in your postsecondary education?
- Monitor the times you say something like, "Who can tell me . . . ?" or "Does anyone know . . . " How might you instead ensure cognitive engagement on the part of your students by rippling your prompts?

Section 2:
Classroom-Ready TPTs

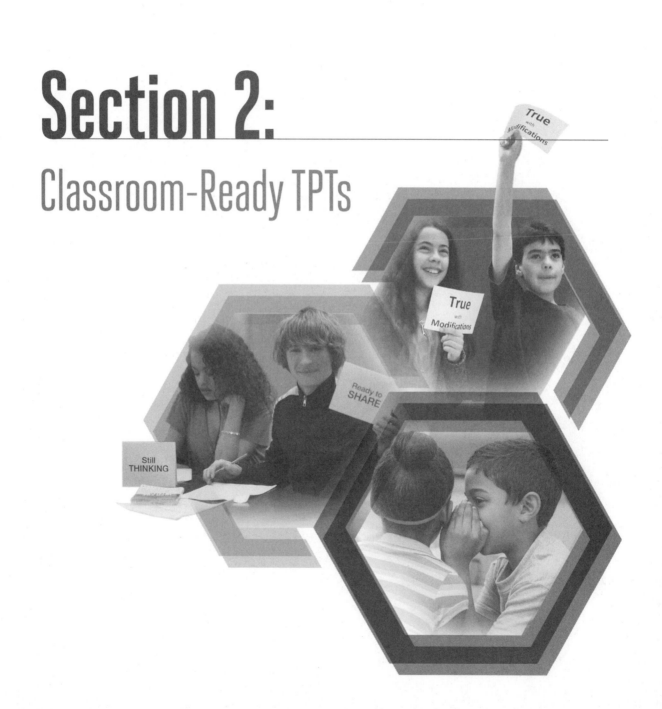

3

TPT Tools and Supplies

I love the idea of having everything in one place . . . already inside the folder and ready to go. . . . I like anything that is this organized, that I can use at a teachable moment in a lesson. It is easy to ask everyone to open the folder, grab the True/False Cards, and then review the new material just covered in class.

Matt Baker, 8th grade English teacher

Once you start implementing TPTs, our hope is that the experiences will change your expectations regarding students' demonstrations of learning. Meghan Babcock noticed this change as a result of her consistent implementation of TPTs. According to Babcock,

> Your expectations change as you start looking at what you call evidence of learning. Thinking about the way you gather evidence, making it more deliberate, sets an overall greater expectation. It becomes a habit. . . . What's neat for me is that when I go into classrooms and generally see teachers calling on a few volunteers, I'm now looking at other kids and wondering what they're thinking, and whether or not they're thinking about the content. Doing the TPTs, you're really finding out what all of them are thinking.

Developing a TPT Mindset

When we think about a traditional question-and-answer session in which three or four hands go up, what does that say about the students who don't have their hands up? Is it possible that only three or four of your students can answer your question? If so, that ought to raise some red flags in your teaching. Start thinking "show me" as you place greater expectations on student participation and on all students providing you with evidence of cognitive engagement. Consider using the posters in Appendix B as quick reminders of no-prep or low-prep TPTs. As you need a quick, unplanned TPT, take a look at the options that are posted.

The TPT Toolkit

One way to make TPTs run smoothly with minimal interruptions is to create TPT toolkits that provide a way for students to easily access the materials that they will need for their TPTs. TPT toolkits can be simple pocket folders or manila envelopes for individual students, or they can be TPT storage boxes or three-ringed zippered pouches that can be shared by a small group of students at a table. If you choose to go with manila envelopes, consider laminating them and then slitting the laminated sealed opening with a sharp tool (only the outside of the envelope will be laminated). Laminated envelopes will last longer than nonlaminated ones. Here are some suggested items to place in your TPT toolkits:

- **A laminated piece of light-colored construction paper**—This serves as a simple whiteboard for students.
- **A flannel square or sock**—This serves as a dry eraser for your construction paper whiteboards.
- **A dry-erase pen**—This can be used with the construction paper whiteboards and is available in thin styles to cause less bulk. You can also try dry-erase crayons that are sold at a fraction of the cost.
- **True/Not True Hold-Up Cards**—These simple Hold-Up Cards work for any content area and can be used repeatedly (see Figure 5.3).
- **Multiple-Choice Hold-Up Cards**—These simple Hold-Up Cards also work for any content area and can be used repeatedly.
- **Emotion Hold-Up Cards**—See Courtney Cislo's sample lesson in Chapter 2 (see Figure 2.1).
- **Decks of paper-clipped Number Cards**—These cards are for hold-ups or for laying the numbers on student desks in response to a TPT (see Figure 5.2).
- **A completed Appointment Agenda**—This chart is useful for grouping students (see Figure 6.3). Student names should have already been filled out. The same agenda can be used repeatedly.

- **The Processing Card**—This card allows teachers to know where students are in their thinking (see Figure 4.5).
- **A laminated hundreds chart**—For elementary children, this chart allows you to plan activities that build number sense. For example, you can have students use the dry-erase pen and the chart to circle 10 less than or 10 more than; circle the common multiples of selected numbers; circle the common factors of selected numbers; circle the prime numbers between two specific numbers; skip count; and do any other activities that build number sense by visually seeing the numbers laid out on a number chart.
- **A laminated A–Z chart**—For early childhood classrooms, this chart allows all students to point to initial, middle, and ending sounds, and to find letters and sounds as directed by the teacher.
- **Laminated content-related charts**—Examples of these are a periodic table of elements chart, a timeline, a map, a metric conversion table, or any content-specific tool you would like students to use repeatedly. The lamination allows students to write on these using dry-erase pens.
- **A smaller envelope with pieces of scrap paper or index cards**—These are useful for Quick-Draws, Quick-Writes, and on-the-spot Hold-Ups, and for recording questions from guided note-taking activities. The envelope will keep these contained and control the clutter.
- **Bounce Cards**—These are useful for facilitating talk between students (see Figure 6.4).
- **Index Cards**—These are useful for ideas like those found in the *TPT Wrap-Ups* chapter.
- **Quick-Write Half Sheets**—These simple tools are one of our most used resources (see Figure 4.1). They allow you to ask students to quickly jot down their thoughts. Because they are precut and include a place for student names and the topic, it reduces the time spent giving directions or asking students to pull out a sheet of paper.
- **Guided note-taking templates**—If you find yourself repeatedly using specific guided note-taking templates from Chapter 7 (for example, Picture Notes, Lecture T-Charts, or Debate Team Carousels), we encourage you to make sets of these for students to have readily available within their TPT folders. This will allow you to use these on the spot as well as for preplanned activities.

- **Tape**—Though you would not be able to include this in an envelope, you may find that you will need to provide students with easy access to tape. Several of the techniques allow for students to post their statements or Quick-Draws, so that they can become a temporary part of the classroom. Providing one tape dispenser for every four to six students will make some of your TPTs run much more smoothly. If you don't have several spools of tape, you can also precut strips of tape and attach them so that they dangle from the edge of a desk in the front of the room. We do this often for our college classrooms, because it is easier than carrying several spools of tape from room to room.

Keely Potter points out that for teachers who do not have a classroom to call their own, TPT folders help them stay organized. As a reading specialist, Potter travels to different classrooms. Leaving the folders in one central location in host classrooms, or traveling with one class set, eliminates the possibility of forgetting to bring materials for planned or on-the-spot TPT activities.

As you read about the various techniques presented throughout this book, ask yourself what should go inside your TPT toolkits. We suggest that toolkits should contain items that you can use with many TPT activities to efficiently eliminate the passing out of papers and unnecessary prep that would be needed otherwise. You may also want to consider purchasing a bell for signaling the end of your small-group sharing times. In our case, we purchased a metal triangle (the small musical instrument). It was inexpensive and highly portable, because it is flat and fits inside a binder.

Thinking Outside the Pencil Box

To be TPT-conducive, you're going to need more than paper and pencils. We have a box with 100 glue sticks that we bring along to workshops and demonstrations. We'll never forget one participant's comment as he reflected on the limitations of one of the examples we demonstrated and how it would never work in his classroom: "It's high school. We don't use glue sticks." This participant's comment may not reflect every secondary teacher's thoughts on resources, but it is indicative of a mentality that glue, scissors, markers, and crayons belong only in elementary schools; that by the time students have gotten to the secondary grades, they have outgrown their need for artsy demonstrations of learning. But as 8th grade history teacher Liz Lubeskie says, "To be good at it, you have to love teaching first and then your content." You can really know and love biology or physics and be completely ineffective at teaching it. Good teaching results in student learning. And if glue sticks and scissors are a way to get students to learn more effectively, then they are never too old to use them. To minimize the time and effort spent searching for supplies, Lubeskie uses "resource boxes" placed at the center of each cluster of desks. These are simple plastic pencil boxes that are just large enough to hold four sets of scissors, glue sticks, highlighters, and one set of markers to be used by four or five students in a small group. We encourage you to use resource boxes, regardless of the age of your students, to enhance teaching and learning in your classroom.

4

On-the-Spot TPTs

You can have the best lesson and read the most intriguing stories, but if you've lost your students, your wonderful lesson wasn't as wonderful as you had hoped. For me that was a huge wake-up call, that one math lesson where I looked up from the overhead and realized no one was with me. See, in my head, it was going great! But it was going great for me, not for them!

Courtney Cislo, 5th grade teacher

Have you ever stopped in the middle of a lesson and wondered whether your students were still with you and whether they were processing or even comprehending what you were presenting? Rather than forge ahead with your presentation, we recommend that you stop and take the pulse of the class as a whole. On-the-spot TPTs allow teachers to quickly gauge the depth of student understanding of concepts being taught. They are activities that require little or no advance preparation. You can insert several in a lesson the minute you notice cognitive disengagement or disconnect. Or you can plan to include them strategically in select spots within your lessons.

As noted in the Introduction, we present each TPT activity in four sections. The first is a general overview of the activity, the second is the steps for "How It Works," the third focuses on "How to Ensure Higher-Order Thinking," and the fourth is titled "Pause to Apply," with reflective questions aimed at helping you to think through how each technique can be applied to your personal classroom situation and your curricular aims.

Think-Pair-Share

Think-Pair-Shares (Lyman, 1981) are an easy Total Participation Technique that you can start implementing tomorrow. For example, 5th grade teacher Mike Pyle uses Think-Pair-Shares several times a day in his classroom. During an observed lesson, he asked students to predict what the main character would do next and be able to explain why. He allowed a good pause, even though hands were going up, and then asked students to share their response with their neighbor.

Think-Pair-Shares were used in most of the classrooms we visited. According to 6th grader Abby, they allowed her to get positive feedback from peers: "I feel very good inside because when someone else hears my thoughts and understands them, then they tell me what was good about what I said." The Think-Pair-Share is a simple but powerful tool that should be used repeatedly and consistently throughout the day.

How It Works

1. Ask students to reflect on a question or prompt. Give them a brief amount of time (perhaps 30 seconds) to formulate a response.
2. Ask students to find a partner or to turn to their assigned partner.
3. Ask them to discuss their responses.

Note: To avoid repeating directions, you can use Pair-Shares as a simple review of procedural directions you have just explained to students. A simple direction such as "Turn to your partner and explain what you have been asked to do first, second, and third" can ensure that all students understand their roles.

How to Ensure Higher-Order Thinking

As powerful a tool as the Think-Pair-Share can be, it is only as powerful as the prompt on which students are asked to reflect. Use prompts that require students to analyze the various points of view or the components that are inherent in your target standard. Ask questions that require students to explain how these components fit together or affect one another. For example, a teacher might ask, "How might the concept of an electoral college be considered undemocratic?" In responding, students must understand the intricacies of the electoral college and then contrast these with the various attributes of a democracy.

Ask students to evaluate something by defending it based on concepts learned. For example, a teacher might ask, "Up until now, multiplying numbers has always resulted in a larger number. Using words and pictures, explain why multiplying by a proper fraction will result in a smaller number." At times you may decide that after pair-sharing you would like students to join their pairs with other pairs, so that each student gets to hear and share with several peers rather than just one.

Pause to Apply

Think-Pair-Shares are arguably the easiest way to get all students discussing the content. If you're not already using them, start planning to insert them throughout your presentations. When might be a good time to try this simple but underused activity? Keep in mind that students will benefit from bulleting or quick-writing their thoughts before the Pair-Share. This simple first step enhances the discussions, because students are given enough time to process their thinking.

⬡ Quick-Writes

A Quick-Write is a brief activity that can be inserted at almost any point within a lesson or planned ahead using prepared prompts. It does not have to take long—just enough time for students to stop and reflect in writing on what they are learning (three minutes is usually sufficient). A teacher might say something like this: "For the next three minutes, jot down your reflections on how the Earth's shifting plates may have directly affected the landscape of where you live." Quick-Writes can also make use of word banks to ensure that students address important concepts learned. For example, teachers can identify a handful of words that they would like students to use within their Quick-Writes. Having a supply of Quick-Write half sheets available for students in an easily accessible location will allow you to save time in asking students to grab a sheet of paper and quickly jot down their thoughts (see Figure 4.1).

Quick-Writes can also be used as a way for students to analyze their own metacognitive thinking processes. Before dismissing his class, 8th grade English teacher Matt Baker asked his students to reflect on the process of conducting their research projects. Figure 4.2 is an example of Morgan's reflection on her own attempts at writing a thesis statement. This process of journaling provided valuable information for Baker as he conducted this quick progress check on his students and responded to each student's status as a researcher.

Figure 4.1
Quick-Write Half Sheets

Quick-Write

Name_____ Topic:_____

How It Works

1. Select a prompt that you would like students to address.
2. Give students a specified amount of time to collect their thoughts and jot down a response (approximately three to five minutes).
3. Follow this up with a Pair-Share, a Networking Session (see Chapter 6), a Chalkboard Splash (presented later in this chapter), or another Total Participation Technique.

How to Ensure Higher-Order Thinking

Go beyond asking students to explain the meaning of a concept. Instead, ask students to make connections between the concepts and their effect on the world around them. Use wide-open questions. For example, get used to using questions that begin with phrases like "In what ways . . ." and "How might things be different if . . . ." Provide opportunities for students to understand the broader implications of what they are learning. Simple questions like "Why is this important?" and "How does it relate to our lives?" might help students stop and reflect on the deeper connections and purposes for what they are learning. Allow students opportunities to interact and listen to their peers as they share their Quick-Writes in small groups.

Figure 4.2
Morgan's Metacognitive Quick-Write

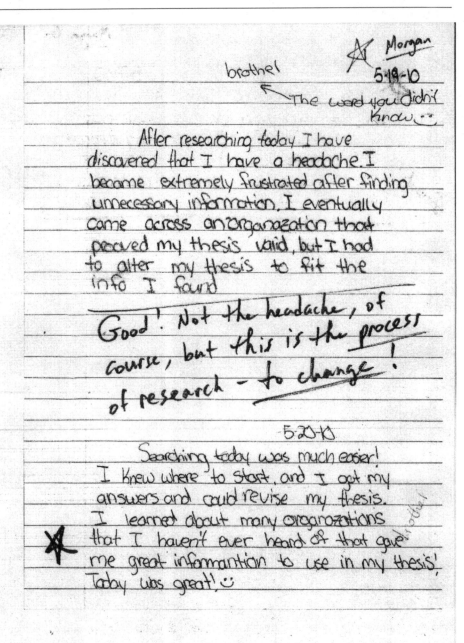

Pause to Apply

Consider having a stack of these Quick-Write half sheets available for whenever you feel that your students could use a moment to stop, reflect on, and discuss important concepts presented. What prompts can you interject throughout your teaching to ensure that students are understanding and making connections between what is being learned? Use a word bank to ensure that target vocabulary or concepts are embedded within the Quick-Write. We encourage you to make the Quick-Write a staple in your teaching. You will notice that many of the ideas presented in this book first rely on students having had an opportunity to process their thinking, preferably through a Quick-Write.

 Quick-Draws

Quick-Draws (Himmele & Himmele, 2009) are opportunities for students to demonstrate their understanding of an abstract term or concept by representing it in a drawing. This TPT can be used with any age group, from young children through adults. Quick-Draws can be used in any content area, not only for concrete vocabulary concepts like *renewable resource*, but also for abstract concepts like *sustainability*. We even use Quick-Draws in our university classes to ensure that students are able to understand and deeply analyze concepts. We are always amazed at the depth and the variety of images that students create as a result of having to analyze and represent abstract theories and concepts in a drawing.

How It Works

1. Select a "big idea" or major concept within your lesson.
2. Ask students to reflect on the meaning of the concept and create a visual image that represents that concept (allow approximately three to five minutes).
3. Have students share and explain their image with a partner, in a small group, or in a Chalkboard Splash (described next).

How to Ensure Higher-Order Thinking

The thinking processes that occur when you ask students to demonstrate an abstract concept in the form of a drawing lend themselves to the analysis of the different components that make up the meaning of that concept, as well as to the synthesis of these components into a visual representation. After students create their drawings, give them an opportunity to share and explain the reasons they chose their particular visual to represent the concept.

Figure 4.3 is Bram's Quick-Draw depiction of the term *vulnerability*, a major theme from Meghan Babcock and Keely Potter's unit on symbolism. In Bram's analysis, he explained that "the Death Star [in *Star Wars*] without the armor is vulnerable. But with the armor, it is not vulnerable." According to 6th grader Hannah, "What helped me out the most was the drawing and writing time [Quick-Draws with accompanying analyses] because it really made me think about the situation."

Figure 4.3
Bram's Quick-Draw of *Vulnerability*

Pause to Apply

If you're thinking that the Quick-Draw would not fit practically within the standards that you are teaching, stop to reflect on the specific topics you will be teaching this week. What big ideas and concepts do you hope students will walk away with? Then think about how you would draw these. We think that most teachers would be surprised with how practical this activity is, even with concepts that don't seem to be easily captured in a drawing. Within the next week, when might you insert a Quick-Draw? Is there a concept or idea that you'll be presenting where it would be helpful for students to pause and synthesize their deeper understandings in the form of a visual representation?

Quick-Draw Gallery Walk

A Quick-Draw Gallery Walk allows for students to share their Quick-Draws and to look for themes and similarities. It requires that students will have first completed Quick-Draws, and it requires that they be displayed around the room.

How It Works

1. Ask students to label their Quick-Draws with a brief explanation as to how it represents the content that was learned.
2. Place cut strips of tape so that they are dangling from a table or have several tape dispensers available so that students can grab a piece of tape to hang their Quick-Draws at eye level around the room.
3. Ask students to grab their notebooks, walk around the room (give them all the same direction, clockwise or counterclockwise), and take notes on the content-related themes that they find in the imagery students have created.

How to Ensure Higher-Order Thinking

Ask students to find two or three new themes that they hadn't thought of prior to viewing their peers' Quick-Draws. Once they've captured a few themes, in pairs or small groups, ask them to create a sentence that encapsulates the imagery in their peers' pictures and the content that it was meant to represent.

Pause to Apply

Once you've tried the Quick-Draw, you may find yourself wishing that there were a way for all students to quickly see and analyze each other's imagery. We encourage you to have several tape dispensers ready so that students can quickly share their images. Have them label the images to make the meanings clear. This activity came as a result of successful shared experiences that we added to our own practice. We encourage you to try it. As noted earlier, you may be surprised at how well Quick-Draws apply to abstract concepts in any content area.

Chalkboard Splash

- "What have you noticed about yourself as a reader because of this unit? Be specific."
- "What do you think the main character will wish for? What makes you think that?"

- "What is the most important thing that you learned about today's topic? Why is it important?"
- "Which of these forms of pest management do you think is the best? Why?"

These are all questions that you could ask students to consider in a Pair-Share or a Quick-Write, but if you want the entire class to see the collective responses of their peers, then the best way to ask these questions may be in the form of a Chalkboard Splash. In a Chalkboard Splash (which can also be a Whiteboard Splash or a Chart-Paper Splash), all the students record their responses (or copy their Quick-Writes or Quick-Draws) onto random or assigned spots on the room's chalkboards or whiteboards, or on pieces of chart paper. After recording their responses, students are asked to analyze peer responses for three things: similarities, differences, and surprises. If you don't have multiple chalkboards or whiteboards, or if you want to hold on to the comments for later reference, use several pieces of butcher paper or chart paper instead of the chalkboards or whiteboards.

For student teacher Heather Berrier, a Chalkboard Splash was a way to wrap up her 5th grade lesson on Paul Revere's historic engraving of the Boston Massacre. After analyzing the event from two different points of view, students were asked to select a spot on the whiteboards and sum up their viewpoint with a Quick-Draw of their own engraving. Before students took their seats, they walked around to look at the various drawings representing their classmates' different points of view.

In the classroom of 5th grade teacher Mike Pyle, the whiteboards were labeled with the names of five different characters from a historical novel being read in class. After students analyzed character traits in small groups, they were asked to write these traits on the whiteboards designated for each character. Similarities and differences were discussed as students explained their reasoning for choosing specific character traits. Chalkboard Splashes provide a quick way to debrief student responses, Quick-Draws, or abbreviated Quick-Writes.

We absolutely love Chalkboard Splashes and use them repeatedly at the university level. They give a "community-of-learners feel" to whatever we teach as students find themselves genuinely interested in what their peers wrote. They are perfect for times when you want to see how every student in the class would respond to a question.

How It Works

1. Create a sentence starter, prompt, or question for which you would like students to see all of their peers' responses (these can also be used with brief Quick-Writes and Quick-Draws).

2. As students generate responses, ask them to copy their responses onto random or designated places on the chalkboards, whiteboards, or chart papers. (We give students a word limit, often 15 words, so that the activity can move more quickly.)

3. Debrief by asking students to walk around, analyze, and jot down similarities, differences, and surprises, perhaps using a form such as that shown in Figure 4.4.

4. Ask students to get into small groups and share what they noticed in terms of similarities, differences, and surprises, before asking for volunteers to share.

Figure 4.4

Chalkboard Splash Debriefing Form

Similarities	Differences	Surprises

How to Ensure Higher-Order Thinking

Chalkboard Splashes are great for addressing the big picture and the relevance factor with whatever topic you are teaching. For example, you may want to periodically use Chalkboard Splashes to address the following prompt: "So what? Why is this important?" Or, for example, what is the purpose for learning about Paul Revere's historic engraving? For Heather Berrier, it was to help students understand that Revere's was one of many views that was represented at the time and that has affected how we view history today. Guide students to analyze their peers' entries. What were the similarities, differences, and surprises? What new questions emerge from the similarities, differences, and surprises?

Pause to Apply

This activity works really well when Quick-Writes and responses to prompts are kept brief. In fact, we will often create a sentence starter and ask the students to complete the sentence in the form of a Chalkboard Splash. For example, after introducing a specific teaching technique in our university classroom, we asked students to reflect on the effect that this technique would have had on their own learning in the mathematics classroom during their K–12 experience. Our sentence starter was simply "In my own experience, the use of this technique would have . . . ." Students completed the statement by personalizing it. What sentence starters could you use in the form of a Chalkboard Splash that will help students personalize or see the relevance in what you are teaching this week?

Thumbs-Up When Ready and Processing Cards

Allowing students to take even a brief moment to process their reflections to a prompt is critical if you want to get high-quality responses—especially if you have students with certain special needs or English language learners in your class. Here are two ways to read each individual's progress as the students process their reflections. Both techniques also serve as great unspoken reminders to students that they should all be in the process of reflecting on the prompt.

How It Works: Thumbs-Up When Ready

1. Ask students to reflect on your prompt.
2. Explain that when they have a thought or are finished, they should put their thumb up as an indication that they are ready to move on.
3. Add a Pair-Share to allow time for students to share what they know.

How It Works: Processing Cards

1. Give students Processing Cards (see Figure 4.5). Processing Cards are index cards, laminated cards, or printed papers folded into "tents" that

on one side say "Still Thinking" with a yellow highlight or a picture of a yellow circle or square, and on the other side say "Ready to Share" with a green highlight or a picture of a green circle or square.

2. Ask students to place the card on the edge of their desk, with the side that says "Still Thinking" facing up or out.

3. As soon as students have completed their task, they should flip the card over so that the side that says "Ready to Share" is facing out or up.

4. Decide on an in-between activity that gives students who finish early an opportunity to apply or extend their learning.

Figure 4.5
Processing Card

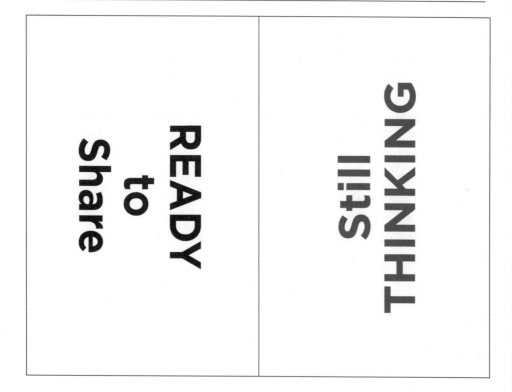

How to Ensure Higher-Order Thinking

Your prompt or task will determine whether or not this activity requires lower-order or higher-order thinking skills. Ask students to justify their responses and to give the basis for their justification. For example, are they justifying responses based on personal experiences or learned concepts? Depending on the activity, both may be valid.

Pause to Apply

Thumbs-Up When Ready is useful for quick activities in which the wait time between the beginning and the end of the processing might be as short as two to three minutes. The Processing Card is useful for activities that take significantly longer, especially when a final wrap-up activity depends on all students having completed a certain task. The Processing Card is one of the suggested items to include inside a TPT folder (see Chapter 3). Having the cards in a folder eliminates the need to pass them out when you need to use them.

 # Similes

Similes compare two unrelated things. For example, a simile using the topic of TPTs might be "TPTs are like safety nets in that they protect students from falling through the cracks." Similes can provide opportunities for abstractly portraying the big picture of concepts in a way that sums up their meaning. To use similes after a teacher-directed presentation, teachers can ask students to make a connection between the topic they're studying and something unrelated. This activity will need to be modeled and scaffolded by first providing examples of similes and asking students to explain why the simile might be true. For example, a teacher might ask students to complete the following statement: "Adaptations are like bank accounts in that ___." Or after modeling the activity several times, a teacher can ask students to create their own simile. For example, a teacher might say something like this: "We've been talking quite a bit about Thomas Jefferson today. I want you to think about and jot down a simile using something you learned about Thomas Jefferson. Thomas Jefferson was like ____ in that ____."

How It Works

1. Create similes using some of the topics you are studying.
2. Ask students to formulate an explanation for how the simile might be true.
3. Ask students to share with their partners in small groups or in a Chalkboard Splash so that all can see.

4. After similes have been modeled a few times, ask students to create their own similes based on the topics they are learning about.

How to Ensure Higher-Order Thinking

By creating similes or explaining them, students are being asked to compare components within both items. In doing so, they are analyzing the topic for which you've asked them to create a simile. This activity takes just a few minutes and can ensure that students are understanding the intricacies or the big picture of whatever you're teaching. Try to come up with your own similes for what you are teaching soon, and see if the students can develop explanations for how the statements might be true. Their reasons may be different from what you originally intended to be the rationale behind the simile, but if their reasons make sense, students have just participated in analyzing the concept you have taught.

Pause to Apply

What are you teaching soon that lends itself to the creation of a simile? Do any similes naturally pop in your mind when you're thinking about a particular topic? If so, use them to prompt your students to make additional connections. Consider reserving a spot on your bulletin board, whiteboard, or chalkboard for the following cloze sentence: "[Topic] was like _____ in that _____." On bulletin boards, add the topic using a separate piece of paper or sentence strip. Or if you are using chalkboards or whiteboards, simply fill in the topic. This is a quick way to allow your students to make analogies between what has been learned and something unrelated.

Ranking

Ranking is an activity that requires your students to analyze components of the concepts that you are teaching and then justify their reasons for assigning rankings. It can be done on the spot, or it can be carefully planned to allow for more thorough analysis. For example, after teaching about the causes for the American Revolution, a teacher might list the events studied and ask the students to rank them in order of most important to least important in leading to the American Revolution. Keely Potter and Meghan Babcock used the Ranking activity with quotes from Kate DiCamillo's book *The Tiger Rising* (2001). They asked students to rank the quotes in order of most descriptive to least descriptive in describing the relationship that was developing between the two main characters, Sistine and Rob. Students were asked to cut the quotes from a handout, paste them in order of significance, and then write out their rationale for selecting the order they chose (see the example in Figure 4.6).

When analyzing students' explanations for their rankings, Potter was highly impressed with the way that one student moved from literal interpretation to an understanding of symbolism. "She's plugging in pieces of the color symbolism. This is the first time she's used it. I think it's through the ranking where they're manipulating the quotes and taking the words out of the book. The ranking triggers noticing the specifics." Ranking requires analysis and evaluation. In the example from *The Tiger Rising*, students were being asked to analyze the specifics in each quote, determine its weight in terms of describing a developing relationship, and then defend their choice.

Ranking can also be used to help students synthesize and analyze what they've learned. After her students learned about the moon and space travel, 6th grade teacher Julie Wash provided them with a list of 15 random items such as matches, an oxygen tank, water, an inflatable life raft, dehydrated foods, flares, a pistol, and a parachute. In small groups, students ranked the objects that they would take based on each item's usefulness if students were going to travel to the surface of the moon. The activity triggered conversations involving what would be needed for matches to work, and whether or not these would be useful to take based on what the students knew about the moon. According to Wash, "The discussion that ensues from the ranking is beautiful because you're forced to make a decision."

How It Works

1. Select items, concepts, steps, events, descriptive paragraphs, or other things that can be analyzed and ranked within your unit or lesson.
2. Ask students to rank them according to specified criteria.
3. Ask students to provide a justification for the way that they chose to rank the concepts.
4. If students are working on their own, allow them to pair-share or network (see "Networking Sessions" in Chapter 6) regarding how they ranked items and how they justified their rankings. Allow them to process what their peers shared and to change the order of their rankings if they've had a change of heart based on new information.

Figure 4.6

Angie's Ranking for *The Tiger Rising*

Angie

The Tiger Rising by Kate DiCamillo

Rank these quotes from most descriptive to least descriptive of what is developing between Sistine and Rob? Defend your choice.

#1

"I know what contagious means," Sistine said. She looked at his legs. And then she did something truly astounding: she closed her eyes and reached out her left hand and placed it on top of Rob's right leg. "Please let me catch it," she whispered. "You won't," said Rob, surprised at her hand, how small it was and how warm. It made him think, for a minute, of his mother's hand, tiny and soft. He stopped that thought. "It ain't contagious," he told her.

Defend your choice: So Rob knows what the Sistine chapel is and Sistine knows what contagious means. She wanted to be out of the bullies way and be with Rob and do what she wanted to do. Thats why she was touching Rob's legs. He probably wanted to tell her about his mom but he just couldn't because that was still in the suitcase..... And they connect.

#2

By then, Norton and Billy Threemonger had spotted them sitting together and they were moving in. Rob was relieved when the first thump came to the back of his head, because it meant that he wouldn't have to talk to Sistine anymore. It meant that he wouldn't end up saying too much, telling her about important things, like his mother or the tiger.

Defend your choice: He wanted to tell Sistine about his life but didn't know how to put it, I guess. he was glad the Threemonger boys came, because then again he didn't want to tell her about his life.

#3

"I know," said Rob. "I know what the Sistine Chapel is." Immediately, he regretted saying it. It was his policy not to say things, but it was a policy he was having a hard time maintaining around Sistine.

Defend your choice: Rob was the only one out of the school that knew what the Sistine chapel was and Sistine was proud of him. he felt like he was meant to tell Sistine abot his mom, the tiger, his life, but he didn't want to. There having a connection.

How to Ensure Higher-Order Thinking

To ensure higher-order thinking, always require that students justify their reasoning. When students in Potter and Babcock's class were asked to rank, they were also asked to justify the reasoning behind their rankings. Students brought out deep metaphorical relationships that were embedded in DiCamillo's book. Even though the use of the concepts of "color" and "suitcase" were not referred to in any of the selected paragraphs, several students pulled out metaphors that had been used earlier in the book to explain the rationale for their rankings.

Sixth grader Emily explained her rankings in this way: "He had his suitcase open, but now it's closed. . . . He got to see things in color for once, not blank. He opened his suitcase and got rid of the 'not-thoughts' for a second." Hannah, another 6th grader, described the bullying by two characters in this way: "Those are the gray actions that help close the suitcase, because the blue sorrow of his mom and the orange curiosity of the tiger almost came out." Students made connections to earlier symbols and metaphors used throughout the book and in book-related lessons. Ranking, and the justification of rankings, requires that students review and then analyze learned concepts together, a higher-order thinking process. Students have to understand concepts beyond the literal in order to effectively justify their rankings.

Pause to Apply

Ranking is one of those activities that would work well in classes from preschool to college physics. What units will you be teaching over the next few weeks that would lend themselves well to the Ranking TPT? Think about analysis as a cognitive process. What would you like your students to analyze within the concepts that you're teaching? Would Ranking be a beneficial way of getting the students to consider *most important* to *least important* concepts learned? Or, depending on your content area, students can rank the *most to least influential, essential, changed, affected, likeable,* or other rankable features of the concepts or characters presented. Consider polling the class or creating a class bar graph of ranked concepts. Use the results as a spin-off for small-group discussions and then a whole-class debriefing.

Numbered Heads Together

Numbered Heads Together (Kagan, 1989/1990) allows all students to be held accountable for being able to relay information that was learned during a group activity. It is a way of ensuring participation and cognitive engagement during such an activity. It is also useful for randomly assigning roles to students within groups.

How It Works

1. Before asking the group to begin their activity, ask them to count off, so that each group member is assigned a number (for example, one through four).
2. It's a good idea to confirm student numbers by asking all of the Ones to stand, then all of the Twos, then all of the Threes, and all of the Fours. This will avoid the problem of numbers not being assigned or being assigned twice within each group. It will also help avoid the possibility of students forgetting or swapping numbers.
3. Inform the students that all group members will need to be able to present their group's information. Wait until after all group work is completed before informing students of the student number that will be presenting.
4. During the debriefing portion of the activity, call out the number for the team member who will be presenting for the group. Because they don't know in advance which person in their group will be presenting the information, all group members are equally responsible for knowing the information discussed, as well as making sure that their peers know it equally well.

How to Ensure Higher-Order Thinking

Steps for ensuring higher-order thinking will depend on the activity that you choose to do once partners meet. For example, if you are choosing to create groups of four for a Hold-Up, then refer to the Hold-Up activity description (see Chapter 5) for ideas on how to ensure higher-order thinking. Also, be sure that you use the first step of the ripple (see Figure 2.2). That important first step allows students to process the content using higher-order thinking and helps them to bring something of value to the group.

Pause to Apply

Fifth grade teacher Mike Pyle has preassigned numbers according to where students sit. He regularly uses this technique to assign students their roles. Often students themselves would make sure the assigning of roles was equitable. For example, during an observed lesson, a student took the liberty of informing his peers, "Number Three gets to write. Number Two wrote last time." This activity can easily be made a staple in classrooms by numbering chairs or desks or simply asking students to count off and write down their numbers. How might you use Numbered Heads Together as a regular staple in your classroom?

Thumb Up/Down Vote

Thumb Up/Down Vote is another one of those quick TPTs that many teachers use frequently. It is simply a yes/no vote with students putting their thumb up if they agree and down if they disagree.

Disclaimer: This simple TPT provides teachers with a quick reading of the class, but to make it meaningful, it should be used as the second or last part of a Ripple (described in Chapter 2). In other words, the vote ought to represent deep thinking that has already occurred, and for which you have already required evidence from each of your students.

How It Works

1. Ask a question for which a yes/no or agree/disagree response is appropriate. Ask students to complete a Quick-Write or to do a Think-Pair-Share where they explain their selection and justify their thinking.
2. Ask students to put their thumb pointing up if the answer is yes or if they agree. Ask students to put their thumb pointing down if the answer is no or if they disagree. You can also give in-between options (for example, thumb sideways if they agree with qualifiers). Before or after this step, ask students to share their rationales for their responses.
3. Don't forget to follow through. If you ask students to vote, don't move on until they have all done so.

How to Ensure Higher-Order Thinking

We almost removed this technique from this edition because we often saw it used as a cheap way to justify getting total participation from all students, when in fact, students who may have been completely disengaged from the lesson could appease the teacher by following the crowd with an up/down vote. Instead of removing it, we decided to use it as an example of a common TPT that works best as the second or last part of a Ripple. The Ripple describes a questioning format that asks students to work individually, then in pairs or small groups, then in a whole-group format. Prior to asking the class for an up/down vote, be sure that they've done the rest of the Ripple. Ask students to justify their responses on a Quick-Write. Link your Thumb Up/Down Votes with a quick Pair-Share in which students justify their rationale for voting the way that they did. Add the in-between options. Rarely is anything black or white. Allow students to put thumbs at an angle or sideways to take the middle road. Practice creating statements that can be either true or false depending on the rationale. The key is that students are able to justify the response that they selected, even if they selected a neutral response.

Pause to Apply

We use this technique regularly in the university setting. We will often present two sides of an argument and ask students to choose whether they agree or disagree with each side. Or we will prepare a true/false statement (that can be either true or false depending on the justification used) and ask students to take a side. After allowing a brief time for students to justify their reasoning individually and then in small groups, we ask students to vote. We'll then ask for volunteers representing the various votes (thumbs up, down, and sideways) to share their reasoning.

With this activity it is important to remember to follow through by waiting for all to vote. We notice that even in college, some students will wait to see whether you're going to hold them accountable for voting before they'll actually commit to a vote. As you think about getting evidence of processing concepts being learned, consider creating true/false statements that can use Thumb Up/Down Votes to get students interested in a topic that has been introduced or that you will be introducing.

5

TPT Hold-Ups

When I'm creating my activities, I'm thinking, "How am I going to make sure that everyone has a part in what we're doing?" Because if you don't actively think about it, then it's not going to happen.

Liz Lubeskie, 8th grade history teacher

Hold-Ups are interaction-based activities that use response cards. In these activities, students interactively reflect on a prompt and hold up a card, paper, or whiteboard in response. Studies indicate that response cards are useful for improving participation and on-task behavior (Wood, Mabry, Kretlow, Lo, & Galloway, 2009); improving students' performance and participation in K–12 settings (Christle & Schuster, 2003; Lambert, Cartledge, Heward, & Lo, 2006); and improving participation, performance, and positive feelings toward their class at the university level (Clayton & Woodard, 2007; Musti-Rao, Kroeger, & Schumacher-Dyke, 2008). Munro and Stephenson (2009) found an added benefit in that when response cards were used, the teacher provided more feedback on responses as compared to traditional hand raising. In a meta-analysis of 18 studies on response cards, Randolph (2007) found that the use of response cards increased student participation, improved student achievement on quizzes and tests, and decreased disruptive behaviors.

Hold-Ups: An Overview

Unlike in other chapters, where each technique is presented along with steps for How It Works, How to Ensure Higher-Order Thinking, and Pause to

Apply, in this chapter we describe the steps for conducting Hold-Ups only once. We do so because all Hold-Ups essentially work the same way, except for a variation in what is being held up. We explain the variations separately.

We have discovered that the most essential component to the Hold-Up is the interaction. Students learn a great deal from each other through their interactions. When students hold up different cards, help them use it as a thinking opportunity for the groups. Let the students explain their thinking to each other, and then do another vote. If students express blatant misconceptions, then insert a quick minilesson before doing the second vote. Be careful not to shoot down student ideas. Often you can help students come to alternate conclusions with a simple statement such as "Tell me more" or a gentle question such as "I see where you're going with that, but is that always true?" For your classroom to be conducive to TPTs, students need to feel safe taking risks. So be sure to validate students through the words you use as well as your facial expressions and body language. When you say something like "I love it! We are growing and learning so much today" after a lively disagreement among teams or groups, it helps students understand that discussion and critical analysis are part of the journey in learning.

How They Work

Each Hold-Up works generally the same way:

1. Ask the students to think about or jot down their thoughts about a set of prepared questions.
2. Before students hold up their cards, have them pair-share or confer in small groups.
3. Say, "Hold it up."
4. Students hold up their cards. Select students to share their group's rationale for their choice.

Depending on the activity, we sometimes modify this order by asking students to hold up their cards before they meet in pairs or small groups. Let students know at what point you'd like them to hold up their cards.

How to Ensure Higher-Order Thinking

Move away from simply looking for the right answer. Use wrong answers as teachable moments, and try your best not to provide quick answers for students who hold up the wrong card. Instead, provide students with an opportunity to explain their thinking, hear opposing responses, and come to their own conclusions through a re-vote. If students are still not understanding, then use that opportunity to reteach the concept while the students are invested in knowing what the right answer should be.

It is important that you intentionally create and embed questions requiring higher-order thinking in your Hold-Ups. Use questions that require students to analyze and make connections between the various components inherent in the concepts you're teaching. Use questions that have no easy answers (see the example using the three branches of government described in the Selected-Response Hold-Ups section). Get students used to defending their responses, especially those that require higher-order thinking.

Pause to Apply

As you read the descriptions of the various types of Hold-Ups, be thinking about which of your curricular aims would lend themselves to a Hold-Up. Students seem to love Hold-Ups, perhaps because the activity feels somewhat like a game. Students love to form a huddle, hold up their cards, and defend their choices. The discussion that takes place as students work together is especially meaningful when concepts are complex, with no easy answers. You'll find that students teach each other as they explain their rationales for their choices. Think about how you might use a Hold-Up over the next couple of weeks to review material and to ensure comprehension of important concepts taught.

Combine a Hold-Up with the Numbered Heads Together (Kagan, 1989/1990) strategy to keep all students accountable (see Chapter 4). For example, you might say, "I would like person Number Three to explain why your team chose that response."

Selected-Response Hold-Ups

Selected-Response Hold-Ups use a selection of relevant choices that are prepared beforehand. Students hold up cards (for example, *Fact* or *Opinion*) as they relate to specific prompts or questions. For very young students, words alongside pictures of facial expressions, seasons, or even simple yes/no cards can be used effectively to cognitively engage all learners. For a lesson on the three branches of government, hold-up cards might include the three initial letters *L*, *E*, and *J*, representing the legislative, executive, and judicial branches of government (see Figure 5.1). Here are some examples of prompts that a teacher might ask for a Hold-Up activity on the three branches of government:

- Which branch is also called "Congress"? (lower-order thinking)
- Which branch has people who are appointed by the president and approved by the Senate? (lower-order thinking)
- Which of these three branches would you say plays the biggest role in ensuring a balance of power? Be ready to defend your answer. (higher-order thinking)

Figure 5.1
Selected-Response Hold-Up Card

Note that the final question takes students to higher-order thinking and requires that they demonstrate a thorough understanding of the interrelationships among the three branches of government. Not all students will agree on the final answer. But the last question would allow for further exploration through researching (perhaps via e-mail) opinions from local community members such as high school teachers, university professors, politicians, people working in the justice system, parents, and any others who indicate an interest in government. Unresolved higher-order questions could be used as a spin-off for highly engaging classroom projects. Consider getting a free e-mail address for your class so that you can bring to your classroom the wealth of understandings present within the larger community (and to protect students from giving out their own e-mail addresses to strangers).

Number Card Hold-Ups

If you teach mathematics, consider providing students with one to three decks of number cards (0–9) paper-clipped together and kept in their TPT folders (see Figure 5.2; see Appendix B for a reproducible version). The number of decks that you will need depends on the activities and the ages of the students you teach. Number Card Hold-Ups offer an added bonus in providing students with increased exposure to vocabulary specific to mathematics. Just for the purpose of visualizing these Hold-Ups, consider the different grade-level curricular aims that could be met using the following prompts and students responding via Hold-Ups:

- Hold up a number that is greater than 6.
- Hold up a number that is less than 3.
- Hold up the sum of 6 and 3.
- Hold up the difference between 6 and 3.
- Hold up the product of 6 and 3.
- Hold up a common multiple of 6 and 3.
- Hold up the least common multiple of 6 and 3.
- Hold up a prime number.

If you teach in the elementary grades, also consider including a laminated "100 chart" (showing all numbers from 1 to 100) in your TPT folders. With dry-erase pens or a crayon, students could circle responses while they look for prime numbers or composite numbers, look for patterns when finding common multiples or common factors, or skip count. If the charts are laminated, dry-erase markers and crayons will wipe off easily with a napkin. We find that the 100 charts are useful for helping children visualize and develop their number sense.

True/Not True Hold-Ups

The True/Not True Hold-Up can be used within all content areas. Again, it allows students to interact and come to a consensus on whether a content-based statement is *True, Not True, True with Modifications*, or whether students are *Unable to Determine* the truth using what they have learned so

Figure 5.2
Number Cards

1	2	3
4	5	6
7	8	9
	0	

far (see Figure 5.3). Consider using student predictions or students' own true/false statements as the basis for the True/Not True Hold-Ups. With carefully created statements, these Hold-Ups can really lead students to understanding the importance of critical analysis. Because very few things in life are completely right or completely wrong, many responses actually end up being true with modifications—especially in the social studies content area, where history is subject to historians' personal perspectives. The more students participate in these Hold-Ups, the more careful they become about analyzing statements beyond simple black-and-white representations. For example, consider the following prompt: "The American Revolution was caused by the British taxation of the Colonists." Students have to really think about that statement. Is there a way to modify the statement to make it "more true"? By thinking through peers' proposed exceptions, students start anticipating and thinking through exceptions, and they take into account the subjectivity of perspective. When appropriate, students can then edit the statements in groups, so that the statements clearly fit into the *True* category.

Figure 5.3
True/Not True Hold-Up Card

TRUE	NOT TRUE
TRUE WITH MODIFICATIONS	**UNABLE TO DETERMINE** based on information learned

You can also have students write the statements on sticky notes to be attached to a chart-paper graphic with four quadrants, labeled *True, Not True, True with Modifications*, and *Unable to Determine*. As the class votes, the sticky notes can be placed in the corresponding areas on the graphic. Any sticky notes that go in the *True with Modifications* quadrant can be edited by the students so that they are made true. As you continue your unit, you can revisit the statements days later, reviewing what was learned or checking to see if students still agree with the statements' placement in the quadrants. The statements that were placed in the *Unable to Determine* quadrant can be revisited as students learn new information. See Appendix B for a reproducible copy of Figure 5.3.

Multiple-Choice Hold-Ups

This simple Hold-Up option requires that you create and project questions from an overhead onto a screen or a smartboard. Students make a choice, confer with their peers, and at your signal hold up their choice of *A, B, C,* or *D* (see Figure 5.4). The letters are assigned to specific options written on the board, depending on whatever concepts you are hoping to teach. The letter cards can be used over and over again because the options will change with each topic you're presenting. What is different about a Multiple-Choice Hold-Up compared with a worksheet or a multiple-choice test is that you can create questions that require students to apply a skill or come to different conclusions and still be right. For example, "Which would you say would be the most practical unit to use in measuring your pet?" The most practical unit depends on the pet. Or they can analyze, come to different conclusions, and still be right based on their own rationales. For example, "Which of these government systems would you say leads to a more peaceful society?" The answer depends on how each student defines a "peaceful society" and the examples used to defend the choice.

Multiple-Choice Hold-Ups can also work well when you want to do an impromptu Selected-Response Hold-Up. For example, with the earlier example using the branches of government, you could simply assign the choices for each of the three branches of government, writing the choices on the board so that students don't forget the letters assigned to each option. Students then would hold up the letter—*A, B,* or *C*—that corresponds with their answer. If you have three options, adding *None of the Above* is often an effective way of allowing yourself the opportunity to throw in options that, when carefully analyzed, don't fit any of the choices. In answering *None of the Above*, students have to really understand the components in each of the choices. As we mentioned at the start of the chapter, what makes using Hold-Ups meaningful is the interaction that ensues as students analyze and debate their choices and defend their rationales for selecting their choices. See Appendix B for a reproducible copy of Figure 5.4.

Figure 5.4
Multiple Choice Hold-Up

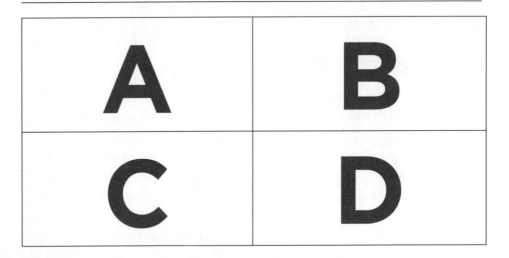

Whiteboard Hold-Ups

The use of individual student whiteboards has become widespread in modern-day classrooms. The benefit in using whiteboards for Hold-Ups is that the possibilities for choices of response are much wider. Students can practice initial sounds, write their thoughts, or show their work in mathematical problem solving. Students then hold up their whiteboards for analysis by the teacher. If you don't have whiteboards in your classroom, you can easily create your own by laminating a light-colored sheet of construction paper. When students use dry-erase markers on these, the answers wipe right off. Laminated construction paper whiteboards are one of the items that we recommend including in student TPT folders. Another creative way of making your own whiteboards is to purchase white plastic disposable plates, which also allow for easy removal of answers written with dry-erase markers. Yet another, more permanent option involves purchasing a large marker board with a glossy finish at a home improvement store and getting it cut into smaller pieces to make a class set of individual whiteboards. Finally, one Ohio school district replaced their desks in the secondary math classes with whiteboard tables. As students work out their mathematical understandings on the surface of the desks, the teachers circulate to see how individual students are problem solving. If the idea seems cost-prohibitive, you'll find do-it-yourself instructions online. And, your traditional shiny desks may work as whiteboards, as 8th grade English teacher Matt Baker discovered (see One-Word Summary in Chapter 8).

6

TPTs Involving Movement

Kids need to interact; they need to process. They need to just pause, think about it, write about it, talk about it, and celebrate it. It's all about celebrating the learning that is happening right now in my head.

Keely Potter, reading specialist

Have you ever noticed how getting up and active gives you more energy to do whatever it is you need to do? Consider a workshop or staff development session where you are so disengaged that your mind is drifting in and out of consciousness. As soon as you are asked to get up and physically do something with what you're learning, you forget how tired you were. Brain researcher David Sousa says there's a biological reason for that reaction. According to Sousa (2006), "The more we study the cerebellum, the more we realize that movement is inescapably linked to learning and memory" (p. 231). Sousa's review of the literature leads him to conclude that

> Physical activity increases the number of capillaries in the brain, thus facilitating blood transport. It also increases the amount of oxygen in the blood, which the brain needs for fuel. The concentration of oxygen affects the brain's ability to carry out its tasks. Studies confirm that higher concentrations of oxygen in the blood significantly enhanced cognitive performance in healthy young adults. (p. 232)

Sousa's insights can be summed up by the oft-repeated phrase "The mind can only absorb what the seat can endure." In light of what we know from brain research, some form of movement ought to be a staple in every lesson we teach. Sousa suggests that "at some point in every lesson, students should be up and moving about, preferably talking about their new learning" (p. 233).

In this chapter, we present Total Participation Techniques that use movement. For these activities, students will be manipulating objects or be out of their seats, interacting and processing their learning together.

Line-Ups and Inside-Outside Circles

A Line-Up is a fun activity that allows students to get out of their seats and share responses to prompts with a variety of people in the classroom. Line-Ups and Inside-Outside Circles (Kagan, 1989/1990) are variations of the same activity. Your choice of which would work best depends on your room setup, because both activities do essentially the same thing. Each allows for your students to be randomly paired with several peers during the length of the activity. The first time you do a Line-Up, students may be a bit confused, but once they figure out how to do it, subsequent Line-Ups should run smoothly.

How It Works

1. Prepare questions or prompts that allow for discussion by a pair of students. When we do this activity, we usually allow time for students to see the questions, jot down notes, and bring their books to the Line-Up to use as a reference.
2. Ask students to stand in two parallel lines of the same length or in two concentric circles. Then, ask students to turn and face the person across from them in the line or opposite them in the circle. You may choose to do an Inside-Outside Circle if you have a large class and students can more easily interact in circles.
3. Ask students to refer to their first prompt and take turns talking it over.
4. Ring a bell or use a signal to get everyone's attention. Ask students to thank their line-mate, and then ask only one of the lines or circles to move two steps to the left so that each person is now facing a different person.

5. As the students are interacting, be sure to move along the lines or circles, listening to student interaction. Doing so will give you a feel for the various levels of understanding as well as provide you with excerpts on which to focus a closing discussion with the larger group.

How to Ensure Higher-Order Thinking

Steer clear of literal or factual questions. Your Line-Up will be a guaranteed flop if your questions require only short answers. In Line-Ups, you want to hear the buzz of student conversations, opinions, and personal or content-based judgments. Use questions and prompts that require students to discuss their ideas, make connections, and justify their rationale.

As you write your questions, think about how the content the students are learning affects them as individuals, as well as the community and the world. What are the implications of the content on life in general? What are the unit's big ideas? Once you have your big ideas, start thinking about the components that lead you to your big ideas and generate prompts from those. Use question starters like these: "What are your thoughts about X? Explain why you feel this way." "In what ways has X affected Y?" Try to get students passionate about the topic without getting too personal or asking for feedback that is politically controversial.

Pause to Apply

In addition to offering the benefit of movement, this TPT is a wonderful on-the-spot option for when you want to debrief student responses to assigned prompts. Think about reflection questions that you have already planned or assigned in class or for homework. How might a Line-Up promote more reflection and interaction in the review of these questions? Rather than simply having students turn in their responses or do a Pair-Share, consider using a Line-Up as an alternative way to debrief your questions and prompts while allowing students an opportunity to get out of their seats and interact.

Three 3's in a Row

Three 3's in a Row is an activity like Bingo, in which students interact with peers and get the peers' feedback on what they should write in the boxes of their template. We absolutely love using this activity, for several reasons:

- Students choose to answer what they feel most comfortable with, allowing other students to get opinions from "peer experts."
- All students, whether expert or not, are required to process the concepts in each of the nine boxes. This outcome is ensured when you require that only the template owner be allowed to write on his or her own template. Each student has to capture what is stated by peers and summarize it in the box.
- It provides teachers with a quick assessment of what the students have learned well, and of what the students need help with. Teachers simply walk around and look for a trend in which boxes are still empty.
- It leads to great conversations that make use of critical thinking (when you ask the right questions).

Figure 6.1 is an example of a Three 3's in a Row activity that is based on the content of this book. If you're reading this book as part of a team, consider using it to spark discussions.

How It Works

1. Prepare nine questions based on the content being learned and type them in a Three 3's in a Row template.
2. Students walk around the room asking peers to explain one answer (only one answer) to them.
3. Students summarize their peers' responses in their box (see *Caution* below).
4. Students then find another peer to answer another question and repeat the process. Students can use a peer only once. This ensures that students are getting around to nine different people in the room.
5. Go over the answers as a class, by asking volunteers to share their responses.

Caution: Don't let students write in each other's template, or you'll end up with a passive game of pass the paper. Instead, by making sure that only the owner of the template can write in the box, you ensure that students are listening to each other, processing what their peers say, and summarizing it in each box.

Figure 6.1
Three 3's in a Row

Find someone who can do or explain what's asked for in the box (one response per person). Ask the person to initial your box and tell you the answer. Then summarize the answer in your box. *Note: You are the only person who should be writing answers in your boxes.*

Provide a definition for Total Participation Techniques. Initials _____	Explain how you plan to implement at least two TPTs that are new to you within the next week. Initials _____	Discuss Paolo Freire's term "listening objects," using personal examples. Initials _____
Explain which TPTs, in your opinion, would do the most to ensure higher-order thinking. Initials _____	Discuss ideal ingredients for a TPT folder that could be used in your classroom. Initials _____	Describe an interesting experience with TPTs and discuss how it enhanced learning. Initials _____
Describe what you believe is the most essential ingredient in a TPT-conducive classroom. Initials _____	Describe how TPTs can lessen the achievement gap. Initials _____	Explain how TPTs might have helped you during your own schooling experiences. Initials _____

Source: From *The Language-Rich Classroom: A Research-Based Framework for Teaching English Language Learners* (p. 152), by P. Himmele and W. Himmele, 2009, Alexandria, VA: ASCD. Copyright © 2009 by ASCD. Adapted with permission.

How to Ensure Higher-Order Thinking

Your activity will only be as good as the questions you ask. Not all of your questions need to require higher-order thinking, but be sure to include some big questions that require students to analyze, synthesize, and evaluate components of the concepts. Think outside the classroom. What are the implications of the concepts you are teaching for the larger world outside the classroom or for the personal worlds of students? Also, be sure to have students complete all nine boxes so that they don't select only questions that address lower-order thinking.

Pause to Apply

This activity can provide a wonderful opportunity for students to interact regarding the content that you are teaching. It takes very little time to create and offers a great opportunity for students to review by sharing what they know well and learning from each other about the topics that they don't know well. How might you use this activity for an overall wrap-up of the units you currently teach? Think about which questions you might ask to ensure higher-order thinking with your students.

Networking Sessions

A Networking Session is a simple mix-it-up activity that allows students to talk to others they usually don't talk to. This activity is wonderful for helping students stretch out of their social comfort zone and for building community in the classroom. Because of the nature of the activity, all students always—regardless of their popularity—have someone with whom to talk. Beth Ferguson, author of the blog *Algebra's Friend*, reviewed the first edition of this book and provided examples of several TPT activities including the Networking Session. The example (see Figure 6.2) provides opportunities for students to analyze various properties of right triangles.

How It Works

1. Prepare one to four prompts or questions. Ask students to reflect on or write responses to the prompts.
2. Ask students to find someone they have not spoken to that day and discuss their responses to a teacher-selected prompt.

Figure 6.2
Beth Ferguson's Networking Example

Networking: Special Right Triangles

Part 1:
Write your responses to these three questions. Write in complete sentences. You'll have five minutes.

Explain why any two 30°–60°–90° triangles are similar.
Write an equation to find the length of a rectangle that has a diagonal twice as long as its width.
What generalizations can you make about special right triangles?

Part 2: When the writing time is complete, you'll share your first response with a classmate. When the music stops, find a different partner and discuss your responses to the next question. Repeat this step with a different partner for each question. Are your answers similar? Different? Do you agree with one another? Do you disagree?

From blog *Algebra's Friend*. Used with permission from Beth Ferguson.

3. After a predetermined amount of time, ring a bell or otherwise signal the class to find someone else they haven't spoken to that day.

4. With their new partner, ask students to respond to a different teacher-selected prompt. Repeat the process until all prompts have been discussed.

How to Ensure Higher-Order Thinking

Use prompts and questions that require higher-order thinking. Go beyond factual questions and instead delve into the implications of the concepts for the world around us. Provide opportunities for students to personalize the responses by applying them to their own worlds. Ask students to defend responses based on learned information. On Bloom's taxonomy, this would be considered Evaluate/Evaluation.

Pause to Apply

This activity is wonderful when preplanned, but it can be implemented as an on-the-spot activity as well. On the spot, it provides students the opportunity to get out of their seats after they have been still for too long. It allows them to process and interact, as they think through a prompt or question that may have originally been intended to wrap up your lesson or to guide you to your next topic. Consider implementing this activity during your next lesson. It is quick and can add energy to a lesson that you feel is in danger of dragging.

Categorizing and Sorting

Categorizing and Sorting can be used to help students understand unique characteristics of concepts as varied as geometric shapes, prime and composite numbers, factors, multiples, and short- and long-vowel words. The interaction among students provides them with opportunities to see how items can sometimes be sorted in different ways and still be correct. History teacher Liz Lubeskie used a sorting activity to help 8th graders determine whether specific items would be considered strengths for the North or strengths for the South during the Civil War. Once the items were sorted, students had to articulate and record a rationale for why they selected the item as a Northern strength or a Southern strength.

In a language arts activity, Julie Wash prepared five piles of books for students to sort according to genre. After a brief content presentation, students worked in groups to sort books according to the specific genres described, and then articulated a rationale for why the books were considered to be a certain genre. The activity was debriefed using the Numbered Heads Together strategy (Kagan, 1989/1990) described in Chapter 4. Students then individually sorted the list of books that they had read that year.

How It Works

This activity will look different depending on what you are sorting or categorizing.

- For categorizing, give students a specific number of items or a list of items. Ask them to sort them into like piles and create category titles based on the features inherent in the groups they made. Ask them to prepare a rationale for describing their category.
- For sorting, determine the names and features of the groups and provide students with items or lists to sort within these piles. Ask them to prepare a rationale for how they sorted.

How to Ensure Higher-Order Thinking

The process of Categorizing and Sorting lends itself to the analysis of components inherent in the concepts being taught. For example, for Lubeskie's students, the sorting of Southern and Northern strengths required an analysis of the content learned and a determination of which side benefited the most from a particular attribute. For Wash's sorting activity, students had to analyze the book's content and determine which genre best described it. Regardless of what you sort or what you use for student-created categories, ask students to prepare a rationale based on what they sorted or how they categorized concepts or items.

Pause to Apply

What are you teaching soon that lends itself to analysis of specific features of concepts that you hope students will learn? Is there a topic that you are teaching that includes specific categories and characteristics of these categories that students should be able to identify? If so, consider using Categorizing and Sorting to help students understand the distinct features between the concepts that are being presented, and ask them to justify their reasoning for the way that they categorized and sorted features.

Appointment Agendas

This is a fun way to get students out of their seats and interacting with others throughout the classroom. Students create appointments with peers by writing each other's names in a specific time slot (see Figure 6.3). When the teacher selects a time, students meet up with the person indicated on their appointment schedule (Ball & Cerullo, 2004). A reproducible version of this figure is in Appendix B.

How It Works

1. Provide students with a copy of an Appointment Agenda with various time-slot options.
2. Ask them to walk around the room and make appointments with various partners.
3. Both partners should select a time that is open and write each other's name in the time slot.
4. If someone remains without a partner, have that person triple up with an existing pair, or offer to be that student's appointment.
5. Once the agendas are filled in, you can use this as a pairing tool. For example, you can ask students to pull out their Appointment Agenda and find their 2:00 appointment and share their Quick-Writes or reflections to a prompt. To create larger groups, have students join the closest pair to form a group of four.

Caution: Partners should appear only once on an agenda.

How to Ensure Higher-Order Thinking

Steps for ensuring higher-order thinking will depend on the activity that you choose to do once partners meet. For example, if you are choosing to pair students for a ranking activity, then refer to the Ranking description (see Chapter 4) for ideas on how to ensure higher-order thinking.

Pause to Apply

Consider using this tool as a staple in your classroom. It is an item that we recommend be included in students' TPT folders (see Chapter 3). Fifth

Figure 6.3
Appointment Agenda

Appointments	
Time	You have an appointment with—
8:00 a.m.	
9:00 a.m.	
10:00 a.m.	
11:00 a.m.	
12:00 p.m.	
1:00 p.m.	
2:00 p.m.	
3:00 p.m.	
4:00 p.m.	
5:00 p.m.	
6:00 p.m.	
7:00 p.m.	
8:00 p.m.	

grade teacher Courtney Cislo uses the Appointment Agenda on a regular basis. "They choose their first six appointments, and I choose the rest. When I pair them, I do it heterogeneously, and it is so cool because they have no idea. It gets them seeing 12 other people, rather than gravitating toward the same person time after time." You can use half-hour time slots to increase the number of possible pairings.

 Bounce Cards

During the beginning of Keely Potter and Meghan Babcock's unit on imagery, metaphors, and symbolism, students struggled to get conversations started.

The Bounce Cards (see Figure 6.4) evolved from a brainstorming session that we had in order to facilitate the discussion among students during that unit. These Bounce Cards went through a series of changes, becoming simpler and less wordy every time they were tried out. The Bounce Cards gave students, especially the more reserved students, something to say. As we circulated, we heard students using the sentence starters as they communicated with each other. During one lesson, Potter instructed the students to form small groups to discuss something about the reading. Without prompting, two groups of three students pulled out their Bounce Cards and moved their chairs into triads and began their animated conversation. It was beautiful.

How It Works

1. Select a student to practice modeling a conversation with you for the class to observe. Practice with that student before modeling with the class.
2. Model the "wrong way" to hold a conversation. For example, demonstrate a conversation that ends quickly once both parties have shared their response, with no back-and-forth dialogue between the two parties. Discuss the importance of conversational skills that allow ideas to bounce from one person to the next.
3. Discuss the following three approaches to responding to peers' comments:
   Bounce: Students take what their peers say and bounce an idea off of it (or extend the idea).
   Sum it up: Students rephrase what their peers say and comment on certain parts.
   Ask a question: Students ask a question regarding what their peers say.
4. Model a conversation using the Bounce Card sentence starters.
5. Allow the students to practice, using prepared topics or prompts.

How to Ensure Higher-Order Thinking

The Bounce Cards provide an opportunity to focus on an important everyday life skill that even many adults are still in the process of developing. Ask students to think about the relevance of developing these conversational skills for their everyday lives. Ask them to try these skills out at home or

Figure 6.4
Bounce Card

Bounce:
Take what your classmate(s) said and bounce an idea off it. For example, you can start your sentences with—

"That reminds me of . . ."
"I agree, because . . ."
"True. Another example is when . . ."
"That's a great point . . ."

Sum it up:
Rephrase what was just said in a shorter version. For example, you can start your sentences with—

"I hear you saying that . . ."
"So, if I understand you correctly . . ."
"I like how you said . . ."

Ask a question:
Understand what your classmates mean by asking them questions. For example, you can start your questions with—

"Can you tell me more about that?"
"I'm not sure I understand . . .?"
"I see your point, but what about . . .?"
"Have you thought about . . .?"

---

during any after school events that they attend, and to bring back news regarding what they noticed. Are conversations with family deeper, longer, more memorable? What do they notice about the relevance of this skill within their own lives? If we can get students to feel comfortable in the art of conversation with each other, it will have the potential of not only building community within our classrooms but also allowing for deeper extended conversations regarding the content that we teach.

Pause to Apply

When you first try Bounce Cards, conversations will be awkward and stilted (maybe even painfully so), but stick with it. The more that students use it, the more the phrases become a natural part of the way they converse.

Ask all students to try the Bounce Cards at the same time, so that no one group of students is embarrassed about trying it out. Let students know that conversations won't sound natural at first, but that the goal is to get so comfortable with bouncing ideas off each other that they will be able to do so without any prompts. Create a larger chart-paper model of the Bounce Card, so that students can refer to the chart without needing to take out their Bounce Cards.

Feature Walk

The Feature Walk allows students to get out of their seats to work in small groups as they analyze important features presented in their textbooks or in related Internet resources. Features refer to pictures, diagrams, charts, maps, sidebars, figures, tables, bulleted lists, and any supports included in the text that aid in the comprehension of the text. These can be pulled directly from your course texts or from related resources. This technique requires some preparation, but once you've tried it, it's an activity that can be saved and reused, with the same or modified prompts.

Before you teach:

- Choose four features from your course text or related resources, and make enlarged (8½" × 11") photocopies of them. Post them on the walls of the classroom prior to the activity. Make sure that the features encapsulate one of the major points or big picture concepts of your lesson.
- Prepare pictures for an average-size classroom (32 students or fewer). You'll need two sets of four pictures so that you can have one group of about four students standing at each feature posted around the room.
- Select a prompt that best fits your overall goal for this activity. You can also select several prompts by assigning and posting certain ones next to their corresponding pictures and features.

Possible Prompts

- What meanings are embedded in this text feature that could not easily be explained using simple text? How does this text feature enhance what you understand about the topic?

- Why would I have selected this picture or text feature as an important one to focus on today? What is the bigger message being conveyed in this feature?
- Who might dislike or disagree with what this text feature is getting at? Why?
- Brainstorm all the people or things that are directly and indirectly affected by the meaning behind this text feature. Tell how they are affected. As you talk, jot these insights down so that you can share them with the group.
- The most important thing about this picture or text feature is . . .

How It Works

1. Place students in groups of no more than four. (The smaller the groups, the more each student will participate.) Ask students to reflect on the text feature and jot down some thoughts as they relate to your selected prompt. After a minute or two, ask the students to stop and share their thoughts with the others in their group.
2. Stop the class and ask all students to move in the same direction (clockwise or counterclockwise) to the next feature posted. Ask them to silently process and then repeat the process of sharing for the new text feature.
3. Repeat until all groups have discussed the features.

How to Ensure Higher-Order Thinking

With the movement inherent in this lesson, it is easy to forget the 30-second to 1-minute silent period where students are first allowed to process and think about each picture or text feature. Tell the students to remind you about it, so that you don't forget this very important processing time. As highlighted in the research that was reviewed in Chapter 2, this individual processing time allows students to analyze the content on their own, rather than having their thoughts funneled into one way of thinking.

Pause to Apply

This technique is excellent to use when you don't want students to overlook important images or text features that can support student understanding of content.

- In social studies lessons, use pictures, data charts, or other salient pieces of information to enhance the deeper meanings in the lessons.
- In language arts, use relevant imagery, quotations, paintings, and artwork reminiscent of the deeper meanings of the era being studied.
- In science, use imagery, current news items, charts, numbers and statistics, and graphics from the book or related resources that apply to the topic being studied.
- For mathematics, use figures, problems, diagrams, and real-life applications that support the deeper understandings of how and why your topic is being taught.

For each set of features (for four features, two sets is enough for 32 students), we attach one of two colors on the top, so that it is visible across the room. When groups move on to the next feature, all they need to do is proceed clockwise to the next paper showing that same color background.

 ## Citation Walk

Similar to the Feature Walk, the Citation Walk allows students to zoom in and analyze citations that are used in a text or in related resources. This technique is interactive, in that students work in small groups, and it requires movement as students circulate to different walls of the room where citations are posted.

Before you teach:

- Select four meaning-laden citations from your text or related resources to post on the walls of the classroom (post these prior to the activity). Your citations should encapsulate one of the major points or big picture concepts of your lesson.
- Follow the directions listed in the Feature Walk technique discussed earlier.
- Select a prompt that best fits your overall goal for this activity. You can also select several prompts by posting them along with each of the citations.

Possible Prompts

- How does this citation address an important element related to the topic we are learning? Why would I have selected this citation as an important one to focus on today?

- What is the author of this quote not saying? What assumptions are being made?
- Brainstorm all the people or things that are directly and indirectly affected by the meaning behind this citation. Who might dislike or disagree with what this citation is getting at? Why?
- What's it *reeeally* about? What is the bigger message being conveyed in this citation? (See Chapter 8.)

How It Works

1. Place students in groups of no more than four. (The smaller the groups, the more each student will participate.) Ask students to reflect on the citation and jot down some thoughts as they relate to your selected prompt. After a minute or two, ask the students to stop and share their thoughts with the others in their group.
2. Stop the class and ask all students to move in the same direction to the next citation (clockwise or counterclockwise), where they will find the next item posted. Ask them to silently process and then repeat the process of sharing for the new citation.
3. Repeat until all groups have discussed all the citations.

How to Ensure Higher-Order Thinking

As noted in the Feature Walk example, students will need time to silently process their prompts. Because citations are easy to capture on paper, make copies of the citations on half sheets of paper or on PowerPoint slides for students to individually analyze prior to their getting up to meet with their groups. Ask them to dig deep into the meaning of the citation to analyze what is being said as well as what is *not* being said, and jot down thoughts so that they are ready to share with their groups. Once they share with their groups, ask them to record two new insights and label them as new insights.

Pause to Apply

This activity is useful for lessons where there are quick and meaty quotations or citations available, either in your text or on the Internet, that carry the potential to convey deeper meanings related to your topic of study. If you can, try to find citations that are written by professionals in the field who are making use of content being taught in their everyday professional lives.

Encourage the students to borrow ideas from one another to enhance what they've already written. Borrowed items can be recorded and cited as "Idea borrowed from . . . ." Help them get used to the concept that there is no shame in learning from one another, and that borrowed ideas should be cited.

Additional Ways to Get Evidence of Learning

The following TPTs are conceptual in nature, so depending on what you teach, you can apply these techniques in a variety of different ways. As a result, we are not presenting these TPTs with specific steps (How It Works, How to Ensure Higher-Order Thinking, Pause to Apply). Instead, you'll find specific examples with prompts to help you think about how to apply these concepts.

 ### Mouth It, Air-Write It, and Other Individual Response Formats

For teachers of very young students who are learning about sounds, blends, and other decoding skills, instead of calling on just a handful to respond to a question, ask them all to do one of the following:

- **Mouth It:** Ask students to silently mouth the response by forming the response on their lips. No sound should be coming out of their mouths.
- **Air-Write It:** Ask students to pretend that they are writing their responses in the air using their fingers. (This works well with initial letter sounds or numbers.)
- **Whisper It to Your Neighbor:** Just as it sounds, ask students to whisper the responses to their neighbor.
- **"Write It" on the Carpet:** Ask students to pretend to write their responses on the carpet using their finger as the pencil. (This also works well with initial letter sounds or numbers.)
- **Show Me with Your Fingers:** Ask students to hold up a specific number of fingers to identify the response. (This also works well with impromptu multiple-choice options. For example, "Would it be (1) a mammal, or (2) a reptile? Show me using your fingers.")

You can get a pretty good feel for students' success in being able to sound out a word by simply looking at how the students' mouths are shaped. A student sounding out the word *cat* looks a lot different than a student sounding out the word *see*. And even if you can't see all the students' mouths, the accountability attached to asking them to show you is more likely to keep their mind on topic than if you call on individuals.

The same is true in math. Asking students to "mouth the answer" is just as effective for a quick on-the-spot comprehension check when you don't have time to gather the whiteboards or number cards. And a student silently mouthing a *four* looks a bit different than a student mouthing a *three*. Fingers work well, too. Asking young students to "hold up a number of fingers that is less than four" will get you a variety of responses and help give you a feel for who is or is not developing number sense and understanding of the concepts "less than" and "greater than." You'll want to model what it looks like to *silently* mouth a word. And just as with Hold-Ups, you'll want to make sure that students don't hold up fingers until you say so, to make sure that students are thinking on their own. Students can also hold fingers up to their chests to provide some insurance against their simply holding up whatever number their neighbor is holding up.

Calling on Someone Is the *Last* Thing You Do

The reminder to use these techniques (e.g., Mouth It, Air-Write It, Whisper It to a Neighbor) ends up being the most common piece of advice that we offer to novice teachers with whom we work. As simple as these techniques are, they come with no handouts or tangible tools that would make it easier for novices to remember to use them. We often find that even the most die-hard enthusiastic teacher candidates who express excitement over using TPTs fall into the dreaded trap of beginning many of their inquiries with the questions: "Who can tell me . . . ?" or "Does anyone know . . . ?" It is important to remember that when we begin our question-and-answer times with a phrase like, "Who can tell me . . . ?" we will end up getting just that—the one or two students who can tell us. Our goal is to teach *all* students, and for that we need to ripple our questions. Using "Mouth It, Air-Write It, Whisper It to a Neighbor" techniques will give us a great deal more mileage out of our instructional time by making sure that all students are attempting to respond. As we explained when describing the Ripple, for higher-order prompts or for times when we want evidence that all are learning, calling on students is fine, but sequentially, it should be the last thing we do.

Acting It Out, Role-Plays, and Concept Charades

Role-plays aren't just for processing stories; they can also work well in content areas like history and science. Acting things out or demonstrating comprehension using the body can allow students to process what they really know about a concept. For example, in science, if you are teaching about the particle theory of matter, you can ask students to quickly get into small groups of three and use their bodies to demonstrate what the molecules might look like in a solid, and then in a liquid, and then in a gas. In a solid they're tightly bonded and slowly moving, while in a gas it's a free-for-all. Students can draw landforms in the air, all at the same time. What might an archipelago look like as opposed to a continent? Have them act out how igneous, metamorphic, or sedimentary rock is formed.

Corbitt and Carpenter (2006) created a role-play activity to better allow thirty 5th graders to understand how the nervous system worked. To introduce complex concepts like motor control, sensory function, simple reflexes, and spinal cord injury, they created a "nervous system game" in which the students themselves acted as messengers carrying messages along an imaginary nervous system. When it comes to science, so many things can be acted out. If you are currently teaching science, think about how the concepts you are teaching might lend themselves to students using their bodies to act out what is happening in the lesson.

Vocabulary also lends itself well to drama. Words produce images. Even fuzzy words that are hard to define (e.g., ambiguous) may be great to act out using facial expressions and body motions. We know a teacher who links every single vocabulary word for the year to a student-created action. The teacher selects a student to act out a word, and then the entire class learns that motion to represent the word. What's amazing is that months later, with little review, students still remember the actions for words introduced months earlier. So instead of asking students to simply define a word, ask them to create and then show you an action that reflects its meaning.

Sixth grade teacher Julie Wash asked students to demonstrate their understandings of genre by playing a game of charades. Wash explained,

> I had the students work in pairs to come up with ways they could
> act out the various genres. . . . Each pair of students chose one genre
> to act out for a spell. When the others had a guess, they raised their
> hands. I told them in order to guess they had to say what genre

they thought it was and what actions pointed to the particular genre. This generated lots of genre talk and really let me see that the students could describe each.

The students' acting included war scenes to describe historical fiction and giving a speech while another took notes to describe a biography. The genres they acted out also included fantasy, nonfiction, poetry, and autobiographies. Linking this charades activity with a Hold-Up using the names of the genres that you're studying adds additional evidence that all students are processing and thinking about the genre being acted out.

As you think about how acting out concepts can enhance the process of learning for your students, don't limit yourself to the examples we've given. Almost anything can be acted out. What concepts are you teaching tomorrow? If you had to act these out, what might they look like? Ask yourself these questions periodically, and you might be surprised to find that even at the university level, almost anything can be acted out. (For example, how would you act out the six levels of Bloom's taxonomy?) The result of students having to act out complex concepts is not only a break from sitting down, but also an opportunity that requires that they analyze the components inherent in the concepts, so that they can assign these components a motion. The activity leads them to higher-order thinking. It's also lots of fun when students are asked to do these in groups.

Simulations

Simulations can have a major effect on students' ability to make connections that allow them to see the relevance in what they are learning. Relevance has become a main thrust for initiatives aimed at stemming the flow of high school dropouts (Klein, 2008; Rumberger, 2008; Young, 2008). Tanner (1990) found that dropouts "objected to particular teachers, teachers in general, specific subjects, [and] the irrelevance of the curriculum as a whole" (p. 80). Eighth grade history teacher Liz Lubeskie often uses simulations to make content relevant to the lives of her students. To help her students understand the feelings of the American Colonists regarding the Townshend Acts, Lubeskie created a simulation, unbeknownst to the students. On the first day that the topic would be discussed, Lubeskie asked the principal to sit in the class to answer student questions regarding the new policies that would be taking effect in their school. On each student's desk was a letter describing changes that would be taking place. "It's very official, with letterhead. I tell them that, due to budget constraints in the economy, the school board has decided that there are going to be some budgetary changes in the school, and that we need to begin charging for certain things," Lubeskie explains. "I tell them, 'The principal is here to make sure I don't give you the wrong information.'" Students discover that these budgetary constraints will result in charges to their lunch accounts for incidentals like desk upkeep, chair upkeep, and other items such as Scantron score sheets for their standardized tests. "I tell them, 'You have a $10 desk rental fee for the year that will be taken off of your lunch account. It's for any desk in the building; you pay only once. It could be refunded, but if anything should happen, if you damage a desk, it will be deducted from the $10.' And 'because of the high cost of Scantron score sheets and paper for tests, we will also need to charge these to your accounts.'"

Lubeskie says that during one of these simulations, the students sat in disbelief and shock:

> They were so livid, I actually had kids stand up and sit on the floor. "There is no way I'm doing that." "My parents aren't going to pay that." I told them, "Listen, I'm just the messenger." That's when they started brainstorming: "Well, what can we do?" "There's nothing we can do." "We can get people to sign a petition, and we can write about it." "We should write a newspaper article. People would go crazy." I had kids calling out, "I'll write it, I'll write it!"

At that point Lubeskie explained that this is how the Colonists felt when they were taxed by the king. She asked the students to tell her how they felt. They responded by saying "Mad," "Angry," and "Frustrated."

"I started writing them on the board. That's when it started to click. 'Is this a trick?'" Lubeskie has used this simulation for several years now, and because students become so emotionally involved, they make a pact not to tell their peers in other classes or their siblings. She tells them, "Would you have understood how the Colonists felt? Have you ever paid taxes? Now, I've got four other groups coming in. Do you want them to feel the way you felt? Then your lips are sealed!" So far, Lubeskie has not had any student spill the beans and ruin the effect of the simulation. For these 8th graders, the Townshend Acts have become relevant.

7

TPTs to Guide Note Taking and Concept Analysis

Often teachers are talking and explaining while students are writing, and the students miss what the teacher is saying because they are so focused on copying the notes.

Mackenzie, 8th grade student

When it comes to note taking, it can be very difficult for students to know where to begin, what's important enough to write down, and how to get the hang of taking notes quickly enough so they don't miss important information. On the one hand, you have students who aren't able to determine how to summarize what is being presented. Instead, they try their best to write their notes verbatim. When Mikaela, a 10th grade student, was asked what she found to be the most difficult aspect of note taking, she stated, "I struggle with writing too much down when taking notes. I need to work on summarizing and putting it into my own words." And on the other hand, you have students who write little to nothing. They either give up or assume that the teacher will stop and let them know when something is important enough to write down.

Research tells us that students' performance can improve with effective note-taking (Lee, Lan, Hamman, & Hendricks, 2008). When students process and repackage what they hear using notes that are in the form of a summary or a visual, they perform better than when they take notes verbatim (Lahtinen, Lonka, & Lindblom-Ylänne, 1997). Effective note taking is a learned skill, and it's important enough that we ought to take time to support students in developing it.

In this chapter, we present TPTs that can help you support students as they summarize content delivered through direct instruction. Within these techniques, we also present steps for helping students pause and analyze the most important concepts presented.

We recognize that there will be times when teachers need to present new information and deliver content through direct instruction. Obviously, this understanding doesn't seem to be lost on the many teachers who end up practicing the stand-and-deliver mode nonstop. This is the type of teaching that results in students becoming "listening objects," as discussed in Chapter 1. But including TPTs in your lessons doesn't mean you'll never deliver new material to students using direct instruction. Rather, it means that during the delivery you'll be stopping several times to allow students to process and interact with the new information being presented. Your goal moves back and forth from delivering content to obtaining evidence that the students are understanding and analyzing the content. Don't you wish your college calculus teacher had implemented these?

Confer, Compare, and Clarify

This activity allows students to read each other's notes, make comparisons, and add to their own notes. Implementing this simple technique can provide several benefits for your learners. First, it gives them the opportunity to pick up tips by seeing how their peers take notes. It also allows them time to reflect on the content, compare understandings with their peers, and ask questions that can be the difference between comprehension and lack of comprehension.

How It Works

1. Ask students to pair up (or assign them pairs) and Confer, Compare, and Clarify. *Confer* refers to getting together and sharing a one-sentence summary of what they believe was the most important part of the presentation. *Compare* refers to students actually getting an opportunity to read each other's notes. They should then compare what they recorded in their notes and what their peers recorded. Let students know that they are encouraged to "borrow" ideas from their peers' notes and add them to their own. *Clarify* refers to students recording any questions that they have regarding what was presented.

2. Ask pairs to join other pairs, forming groups of four, and share questions (from the Clarify piece).
3. Ask students to record the questions that could not be answered in the larger groups of four on the board in a Chalkboard Splash (see Chapter 4), or they can record these questions on scrap paper or index cards.
4. Address the questions that were recorded before moving on.

How to Ensure Higher-Order Thinking

Use prompts to help students analyze the effectiveness of their own note taking. Ask them to analyze whether or not the notes they recorded capture the most important pieces of the presentation. Ask whether or not they have picked up any note taking tips from their friends. Remind students that effective note taking is a skill that will take time and practice to develop. Ask them to analyze and reflect on the process of note taking. What was one thing they did well and one thing that they would like to work on for the next portion of the presentation? Ask students to jot down their area for improvement in the margin of their notes, or ask them all to write it on the board in a Chalkboard Splash.

Pause to Apply

This is a great on-the-spot activity that you can apply right away, with no preparation. Think about how this simple technique might have enhanced the understanding of content you may have presented recently. How might you use it in the future? As students are using Confer, Compare, and Clarify, circulate to make sure they are capturing the most important pieces of the presentation. Before moving on to the next topic, allow a few students to share what they wrote.

Graphic Organizers and Prepared Packets

Konrad, Joseph, and Eveleigh (2009) conducted a meta-analysis of eight peer-reviewed studies that looked at the role of "guided notes," or teacher-prepared handouts with cues and spaces for students to fill in key information during a lecture. In these studies, guided notes positively affected learning and note-taking accuracy. The researchers concluded that "guided notes provide students with a model for taking accurate and complete notes" (p. 442). For every unit she teaches, 8th grade teacher Liz Lubeskie prepares guided notes in the form of unit packets with various teacher-made graphic organizers that include causal charts, time lines, and other visual maps to guide students through the presentations that she prepares. Graphic organizers are aimed at helping students record information in a way that visually supports their understanding. Figure 7.1 is an example of a graphic organizer that we used in our earlier book. It is aimed at helping students understand causal links between historical events and their relevance for today.

How to Ensure Higher-Order Thinking

At some point during your lessons, prompt your students to connect the learning to the world around them. What are the content's implications for their world? Lubeskie leaves a two-inch footer on all of her handouts so that the students can do a final Quick-Write in response to a prompt. Each cluster of desks has a pencil box holding scissors, glue sticks, and markers. After responding to the prompt, students pair-share and then grab the scissors, cut the footer off, and hand it to Lubeskie before leaving. Consider using footers as a way to address the big ideas in your lessons. Doing so reduces the need for extra papers or index cards.

Anticipatory Guides

The idea for Anticipatory Guides has been circulating in educational arenas for many years. Nonetheless, these guides can provide a wonderful way to introduce new material to students. They are easy to create, provide a pre-assessment for content being presented, and allow students to actively process their predictions to true/false statements about the content to be learned (see the example in Figure 7.2).

How It Works

1. Create true/false statements related to the content you will be presenting.

Figure 7.1
Graphic Organizer

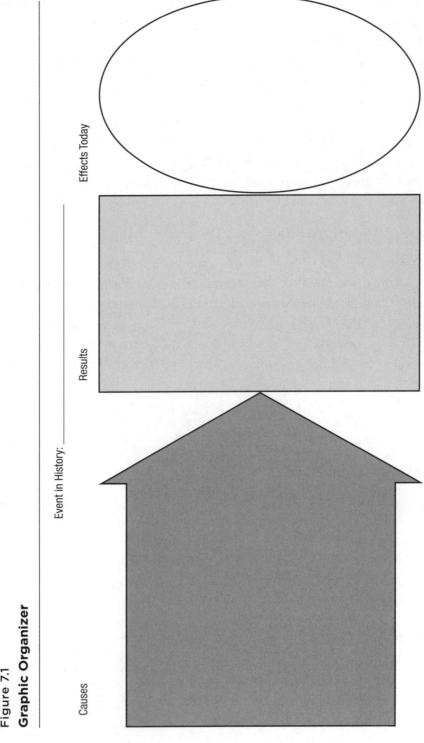

Event in History: _____

Causes

Results

Effects Today

Source: From *The Language-Rich Classroom: A Research-Based Framework for Teaching English Language Learners* (p. 64), by P. Himmele and W. Himmele, 2009, Alexandria, VA: ASCD. Copyright 2009 by ASCD. Reprinted with permission.

2. Ask students to read the statements and predict the responses based on what they know about the topic or related topics. Answers should go in the "Before" column.

3. Ask students to pair-share their responses and explain their rationales for choosing the answer they did. Ask them to develop any questions that can be brought to the class as a whole.

4. You can either debrief this activity by taking Thumb Up/Down Votes as you go over the facts related to each statement, or you can have students hold onto their Anticipatory Guide and address each statement as it comes up in your unit (see Pause to Apply).

How to Ensure Higher-Order Thinking

Write your statements so that the responses are not clearly true or false for someone who knows very little or nothing about the content. Stay away from "giveaway" statements by being careful not to use the terms *always* or *never.* Your goal should be to allow students to think and make connections from what they know to what you will be introducing, and to have them genuinely evaluate whether the statement may be true or false. Also, consider using statements that can be both true and false depending on the rationale used for defending the answer.

Pause to Apply

Anticipatory Guides can be used as a prereading activity, as a way of introducing a topic, or as a pre-unit activity. As the unit progresses, revisit the statements in the guide. For example, "Now that you've been presented with more content, let's take a new vote using thumbs up/thumbs down." At the end of the unit, allow time for students to fill in the "After" column on their guide.

Picture Notes

Picture Notes can provide an excellent way for students to stop and process what they have learned. They are meant to accompany written notes, not to completely replace them. During selected pause points, students create a picture that illustrates the concepts being learned. For example, during their first "picture-pause," students might be asked to illustrate the first of three theories on what causes inflation. To draw a picture, students have to effectively consolidate the concepts presented and then be able to explain

Figure 7.2

Anticipatory Guide for the Revolutionary War

Before	Statement	After
True and/or False	Most of the American Colonists considered themselves patriots.	True and/or False
True and/or False	Loyalists wanted to remain loyal to Britain.	True and/or False
True and/or False	The Continental Congress was a branch of government overseeing the affairs of the North American continent.	True and/or False
True and/or False	The Declaration of Independence was drafted and signed before the Colonists went to war.	True and/or False
True and/or False	The Boston Massacre was an event that resulted in the death of thousands of Colonists.	True and/or False
True and/or False	The Boston Tea Party is an event held annually to celebrate the fact that Bostoners could finally import and purchase tea.	True and/or False

their picture to a peer. For students who have only a partial understanding of what has been presented, the sharing is essential, because students get to add to each other's understandings in between each picture-pause. These picture-pauses, and the accompanying interactions, add to each student's final understanding of the "big picture" drawn in the final box.

Eighth grade teacher Liz Lubeskie uses Picture Notes to ensure comprehension of concepts being presented. For example, she asks her students to create pictures that represent the three parts of the Townshend Acts:

> I give them the titles and ask them to draw pictures, and that's how they remember their Townshend Acts. The next day, I ask them to redraw the Townshend Acts without looking at their notes, and the pictures end up being almost identical to the ones drawn the day before. So they do remember what they drew without even looking at the pictures.

How It Works

1. Select strategic pause points during your presentation—points when students will stop, process what they have learned, and draw a picture that illustrates these concepts. Be sure to emphasize that skill in drawing is not what is important. The picture-pause and the sharing can be limited to about four minutes.

2. Ask students to share their picture with a peer (preselected or randomly selected) and to keep track of any questions they have. Circulate to get a feel for whether or not students are comprehending the topics presented.

3. Address any questions that emerge from the picture-pause.

4. Toward the end of the lesson, ask students to consolidate what they've learned into a final drawing that captures the "big picture," along with a summary statement below the picture.

5. You can debrief the big picture portion in a Chalkboard Splash (described in Chapter 4) and a search for similarities, differences, and surprises, or in a small-group discussion, followed by individuals sharing their big picture.

Figure 7.3 is a template that can be used for recording Picture Notes. But Picture Notes can also easily be drawn right inside student notebooks during assigned pause points.

How to Ensure Higher-Order Thinking

Don't limit Picture Notes to concrete things that can be drawn relatively easily. When students visually represent concepts presented using pictures, they have to wade through information and consolidate this into an image. Encourage students to use symbolism to capture concepts that are abstract as well as concrete. When you notice that a student excels in capturing some of the more abstract concepts in his or her Picture Notes, ask that student to share the Picture Notes with the class and to explain the symbolism behind them. Ask students to create a final Picture Note that addresses the "big picture" of the lesson and then to explain it with a caption.

Pause to Apply

If you haven't yet taken the opportunity to have students visually represent their thoughts in the form of drawings or graphics, try it. These work in many different contexts. Consider the lessons that you will be teaching over the next week or two. If you were to divide a lesson into two or three parts, how could each of those parts be captured visually? What is the overall big picture of the lesson? Try it first on your own and then assign it in class. Bring along your pictures, so that after the students share their pictures, you can show them how you also visually represented the concepts.

Lecture T-Chart

A Lecture T-Chart (see Figure 7.4) can be very useful to students by allowing them to review their notes and sum them up on the right-hand side of the T-chart using words or a Quick-Draw. They can take notes in the left-hand column and then, during a pause point, sum them up in the right-hand column. The T-charts can also serve as a reminder to teachers to pause and give students time to summarize their thinking.

How It Works

1. During the presentation, students take notes in the left-hand column.
2. Periodically stop (at several pause points) to allow students to read over their notes and summarize them in the right-hand column.
3. Allow time for pair-sharing summaries and for recording questions on index cards or in a Chalkboard Splash.
4. Allow time to answer any questions that students have.

Figure 7.3
Picture Note Template

Picture-Pause #1	Picture-Pause #2	Picture-Pause #3
Topic	Topic	Topic
The BIG Picture		
Explanation:		

How to Ensure Higher-Order Thinking

Go a step further: after you ask students to summarize the most important concepts discussed, ask them to predict what's coming next in the presentation. Or ask students to reflect on what they think the implications of the content might be for their world today. Ask students to designate a spot in their notes to address the "So what?" and the relevance question. For example, "Why do you think invasive species matter to us?" Give them time to share their thoughts in small groups before addressing this point in the presentation.

Figure 7.4
Lecture T-Chart

Notes	Sum It Up

Pause to Apply

The practice of stopping to allow students to review and summarize their notes is a great habit to develop. Several of the activities in this chapter provide a variation on this theme. Think about using the T-chart in Figure 7.4 or simply asking students to create a larger right margin in their notes where they can sum up the most important concepts that they will be writing about. Don't forget to pause and remind them to summarize what has been presented. As noted in the research cited earlier in this chapter, students who can summarize their notes rather than copy them verbatim will have a better grasp of what was presented. But this skill takes time and practice to develop. For students who struggle with writing and who need help summarizing their notes, this simple T-chart can be a reminder for both you and the students to pause, review the notes, and summarize what was presented.

⬡ Reflection Logs

For teacher-directed presentations, Reflection Logs allow for breaks where students can pause to process content during presentations that are heavily teacher directed.

How It Works

1. Divide up your lesson into logical sections. Create a template that includes pause points where students will process portions of the content right after it has been presented (see Figure 7.5). Students can submit these to the teacher for a quick review, or keep them with their notes.
2. Stop the lesson at every pause point, and ask students to take two to three minutes to provide a brief written summary and explain the relevance of what was presented.
3. Ask them to stand up and pair up with someone they haven't spoken to that day and share their reflections.
4. After about two to three minutes, ask for a volunteer or two to share their reflections.
5. Students can then sit down until it is time for the next reflection pause.

How to Ensure Higher-Order Thinking

When reflecting on content that has several new concepts, such as that shown in Figure 7.5, ask students to be selective and specific. What are the two most important things that they learned? Or when reflecting on presentations that are more narrative in nature (e.g., history, language arts), ask them to think about the importance of what is being learned. What are the implications of what is being learned? Instead of simply retelling the content, which they will have already done in their notes, ask them to think about its relevance and why it matters.

Pause to Apply

During what portions of your curricular presentations do you find yourself talking too much? In what assessments of content do you find that students don't always grasp what you're trying to teach? These may be areas

Figure 7.5
Reflection Log

Digestion

Pause Point #1 The Mouth

_____

_____

_____

Pause Point #2 The Esophagus

_____

_____

_____

Pause Point #3 Mechanical Digestion

_____

_____

_____

Pause Point #4 Chemical Digestion

_____

_____

_____

Draw the process on the back of this sheet.

that would benefit from simple checkpoints like those offered using reflection logs. Try dividing up your content presentations into soluble portions, and using reflection logs to support student processing. Keep in mind that this technique can lose its impact if it is overused. Reserve its use for when content presentations are more intense and teacher directed.

Pause, Star, Rank

Have you ever written yourself a note and gone back to it days later, only to find that you had no clue why you wrote it or what you were thinking of when you wrote it? This activity allows students to review their notes while the concepts are still fresh in their minds. They can clarify what they wrote while they still remember why they wrote it. They also can encode their notes with stars to indicate the most important concepts, and then with numbers indicating the ranking of the three most important points.

How It Works

1. At the end of a teacher-led presentation, ask students to review their notes and place stars next to the most important concepts.
2. Select the three most important concepts and create a summary sentence for each concept.
3. Rank the three summary sentences in order of importance, placing a *1* on the most important, and a *2* and a *3* on the next two most important concepts.
4. Allow students to share what they starred and ranked in small groups; then as a whole group, or as a Chalkboard Splash, record their top-ranked concept (in the form of a summary sentence).

How to Ensure Higher-Order Thinking

This activity lends itself to analysis. By having students read over their notes and determine the importance of what they've read, students are analyzing the concepts on which they took notes. By following this up with a top-three ranking, you are further requiring the students to analyze, because unlike the starring component, the ranking forces them to choose and rank only the three most important concepts. For those students who might tend to place a star on nearly everything they write, this is a final way to require analysis.

Pause to Apply

This is an excellent wrap-up activity that is perfect when you have a few minutes left at the end of your presentation. It is simple to do and can be planned or implemented on the spot. At the end of this activity, allow time for students to make any additions to their notes once they have thought about what their peers selected.

We have also used this activity when wrapping up themes or units of study. After asking students to review several days' worth of notes, Quick-Writes, and in-class activities, we ask them to rank the six most important concepts discussed. This is a simple way to close the unit before beginning a new one.

Key-Word Dance

A Key-Word Dance is another activity that allows students to review their notes while the notes are still fresh in their minds. Using this technique, students review their notes and select words that they feel are essential to understanding the concepts. Once they've selected the key words, they make them "dance" by writing the words in the form of a poem. For example, using one of the journaling pages from Babcock and Potter's *The Tiger Rising* unit on symbolism (see Chapter 2), this Key-Word Dance was created using Emily's notes from 6th grade:

He has his . . .
Feelings
Inside
-His Color
-His Purpose

He is . . .
Blank

So, he sees . . .
People

And Things
In Blank Too

How It Works

1. After a teacher-led content presentation, ask students to review their notes and underline a specific number of words from their notes (perhaps 15 to 20) that they believe are important for understanding the content.
2. Ask the students to use the words to create a Key-Word Dance. Encourage them to use repetitive phrases to add to the poetic feel of the writing. (Model the activity before asking students to do it.)
3. In small groups, ask them to share their poems and explain why the words they chose are representative of the big ideas presented.
4. Ask volunteers to share as a whole group or in a Chalkboard Splash.

How to Ensure Higher-Order Thinking

Key-Word Dance is another activity that allows students to use analysis to determine words that are important for understanding the concepts on which they have taken notes. As students are analyzing their notes, they are participating in higher-order thinking. Don't forget to ask students to defend their reasons for choosing the words that they selected. Also, allow them time at the end to add any key words that they'd like to "borrow" from their peers.

Pause to Apply

This activity will require modeling. But once students get the hang of it, it could also be considered an on-the-spot TPT wrap-up. Before using this with your class, ask to borrow a student's notebook and take a few minutes to model this activity using notes the student has recently taken. Then be sure to circulate to support students as they select their important concepts and words.

 # Debate Team Carousel

Debate Team Carousel is an activity in which students debate a position from various angles as prompted on a template (see Figure 7.6). It allows students to see various aspects of an issue and consider what the opposing and supporting arguments for a certain position might be. For example, an art teacher might ask, "Do you think Picasso was a more skilled painter before or after he discovered cubism?" In a Debate Team Carousel, this question would lend itself to requiring students to eventually analyze the loaded meaning of the term *skill* from different angles. This activity works with groups of four or more. Once all four boxes are filled in, the papers are returned to the original owner.

Twelfth grade teacher Melanie Upton asked students to use a Debate Team Carousel to review their editorial essays. Students were asked to summarize their editorials in the first box, and peers commented by responding to the prompts. During the debriefing discussion, several students expressed appreciation that their peers had raised opposing issues that the editorial writers hadn't yet thought about and that would need to be raised and addressed in the editorial in the form of rebuttals. The Debate Team Carousel was also used in Krista Grimm and Susan Hagel's 3rd grade co-taught classroom. Students used Bounce Cards as a scaffold to help them write their responses based on the template's prompts.

How It Works

1. Create a prompt that requires students to use their judgment and the content presented to take a position. Record the prompt on the board or have it ready in your slides, so that students can read and refer to it while they complete all the boxes in the template.

Figure 7.6

Debate Team Carousel

1. Give your opinion and explain your rationale. Record your opinion and explain your reason for it.	2. Add a supporting argument. Read your classmate's response. In this box, add another reason that would *support* your classmate's response.
3. Add an opposing argument. In this box, record a reason that might be used to argue *against* what is written in boxes #1 and #2.	4. Add your "two cents." Read what is written in the three boxes. Add *your opinion* and *your reason* for it in this box.

2. You will need a template for every student, so that all are responding at the same time. Ask all students to record their judgment and a rationale for what they believe in the first box.

3. Ask all students to pass their papers to the right, and read and add a supporting rationale that goes along with their peer's judgment (even if they don't agree).

4. Ask all students to pass their papers to the right, and read what is in both of their peers' boxes and add something that might be used as an opposing rationale (whether they agree with the rationale or not).

5. Ask all students to pass their papers to the right and add their own opinion, supporting it with their rationale, in the final box.

6. Ask students to give the papers back to their original owners.

7. Ask volunteers to share with the class some of the arguments for and against on their carousel forms.

How to Ensure Higher-Order Thinking

The Debate Team Carousel lends itself to the analysis and evaluation of a topic. Be sure not to spell out the arguments for and against. Although the presentation of the content will usually take a slant toward one position or another, be careful not to explicitly tell students, "These are the arguments for, and these are the arguments against." Let the students come to their own judgments based on learned content. Students will also have to consider and record what they believe might be supporting as well as opposing views. In doing so, they are required to analyze and evaluate learned material from different perspectives. Rationales for and against can be summarized when you debrief the activity in a whole group.

Pause to Apply

Think about how you might use this activity in your particular content area. To get you started, here are a few examples:

- In science, questions used with Debate Team Carousels can focus on applying the content that students have learned to the real world around them. For example, "Now that we've talked about the impact that birdfeeders can have on the ecology of birds, should the use of birdfeeders be banned?" "Do you believe that our country should spend money to help avoid man-made environmental disasters, or do you think the money should go to respond to the disasters after they happen?"

- History lends itself to debate. For example, a teacher might use these types of questions during a Debate Team Carousel: "Do you think nationalism did more to unite the country's citizens or to divide them?" "Do you think that it is *undemocratic* not to vote?"

- In language arts, yes/no questions can be used with this activity to evaluate the literature that is being read. For example, "Do you think that Rob should trust Sistine with the things that are in his *suitcase*?" Support your responses with examples from the text.

Consider having a pile of these templates on hand for those teachable moments when someone says something intriguing or asks a question that you feel would be a good prompt on which to base a Debate Team Carousel.

Cut-and-Pastes

Who said Cut-and-Pastes were just for kindergarten? In our opinion, they can be used effectively with everyone from preschool to adulthood. This hands-on activity of manipulating concepts, analyzing them, and moving them around would work whenever students are being asked to understand characteristics of a specific number of concepts with distinct principles that apply to each. For example, with younger children they might be used to match synonyms or antonyms, or to paste on prefixes or suffixes. With adults, for example, we use Cut-and-Pastes to better understand things like Bloom's taxonomy, assessment concepts, and linguistic concepts. For the next two TPTs, we will be embedding the procedures and the "Pause to Apply" information within the descriptions.

Keely Potter and Meghan Babcock combined the Ranking TPT with the Cut-and-Paste. They selected excerpts from the text and asked students to rank them from the one that best described the developing relationship between the two main characters, to the one that least described the developing relationship (see Figure 4.6 in Chapter 4).

How you structure a Cut-and-Paste depends largely on what you're teaching. But in the case of, for example, prefixes and suffixes, a specific number of prefixes and suffixes could be prepared for attaching to root words. Suffixes like *able* or *ful* and prefixes like *un* and *anti* could be pasted onto root words to change the meanings. You can add a challenge for students to use as many prefixes and suffixes as they can, using the fewest root words. This will challenge them to add both suffixes and prefixes to single root words: *dis-agree-able*, *un-friend-ly*. These activities are even more fun to do in small groups, where students can put their brains together to meet the challenge set for them. When we assign Cut-and-Paste activities in class, we usually hear a hum of activity, as students cut their pieces and manipulate them back and forth, justifying why their placement in a specific spot might be the best alternative. Circulating and catching a comment here and there as we listen to students learning from each other is a wonderful experience.

When you have Cut-and-Pastes that include specific options that describe distinct concepts, toss in options that might fit into more than one category. This approach will ensure that your students are using higher-order thinking as they interact. It will encourage students to talk and to develop a rationale for why their choice makes sense to them. Ask students to justify. This requirement also establishes the notion that things are not always simple to categorize. The example in Figure 7.7 (p. 112) is a Cut-and-Paste sorting activity that requires students to analyze who would most likely have made specific statements (*Patriots, Those Who Were Neutral*, or *Loyalists*). It contains options that could fit in several columns. Note the student's justifications for selecting the placements she chose.

Will you be teaching anything soon that might lend itself to a Cut-and-Paste? Sometimes the simple novelty of adding glue and scissors to concept development offers a much needed break from the mundane and allows you an opportunity to quickly gauge student understandings. Consider adding this TPT as a way to enhance student understandings of any set of concepts with distinct features.

TPTs During Read-Alouds

It's always sad to hear about the lack of read-aloud time set aside for children in schools. Even as early as 3rd grade, it's common to hear that the chapter book read-aloud no longer exists. Its rank on the list of academic priorities is often so low that some teachers have relegated read-aloud time to the same time assigned to classroom bathroom breaks. The distraction of students walking in and out of the room is such that those in class are not even paying attention to what is being read. But even though the results are not easily quantifiable, read-alouds are valuable for building what we call "peripheral language," or academic language (vocabulary, grammar, style) that students begin to understand within a meaningful context (Himmele & Himmele, 2009). With repeated exposure, peripheral language becomes active language that the students not only understand but actually use.

Read-alouds play a vital role in building children's language long before they even enter formal schools. Studies show that the read-aloud experience and vocabulary development are closely linked (Meehan, 1999; Roberts, 2008; Sénéchal & LeFevre, 2002; Sharif, Ozuah, Dinkevich, & Mulvihill, 2003). It ought to concern us that the read-aloud is getting less and less attention, often as a result of pressure to raise scores for students who probably could most benefit from the contextually rich vocabulary found in read-alouds. This is particularly true because access to read alouds is not equal across

Figure 7.7

Gabriela's Cut-and-Paste

Who Said That?

Decide whether the statement would most likely be made by a Loyalist, Patriot or Someone who is Neutral.
Cut and place the statement in the column it most likely belongs.

Patriot	Neutral	Loyalist
No taxation without representation!	This war has nothing to do with me! I am not now, nor have I ever been British!	These peasants ought to be grateful that they are even included among the British citizenry.
Give me liberty or give me death!	Yes, we have certainly suffered! However, peace, not war is the answer. Certainly we have not exhausted all of our attempts at a peaceful reconciliation.	What will happen if the war is lost by the colonies? Will I lose my land, my business? Yes, of course I will. I will become the detested one who refused to support the cause.
My heart is here. This is my home now. And I will fight to make it what I wish for it to become.	I'm torn. I fear that the war will do nothing more than tear this region apart. I fear for my children, for my children's children. War is not the answer. But, neither is doing nothing.	I am a subject of King George. Independence is nothing more than treason! That word will not be spoken in my home.
These laws violate my rights. I am just as much a British citizen as are those who remain in Britain.	We have no defense against Britain's vast army. And, even if we were to defeat Britain, what then? How will we protect ourselves from others who want to destroy us? Will Britain come to our rescue after we have so blatantly shot at them?	For the safety of my family, my dear children, I have no alternative but to return home.

[Handwritten annotations: "Because they don't want to fight, but they don't just want to sit around." "this could go in any of the boxes" "Please explain why you think so." "this could also go in loyalists because they don't want to fight."]

socioeconomic boundaries. "It has been estimated that young children in high-poverty environments are read to out of storybooks about 25 hours before entering school, as compared to 1,000+ hours of reading aloud to children in non-poverty homes" (Reutzel & Cooter, 2015, p. 117).

Children learn language from hearing it in contexts that they understand. Storybooks often contain a mix of conversational and academic language embedded within enjoyable contexts that make it easy for children to understand. Because oral language development and vocabulary are fundamental to reading success, the read-aloud time helps level the playing field. It ought to be considered sacred time, and it ought to be protected. We also strongly believe that students are never too old to have someone read to them. And they're never too old to enjoy the benefits of the language acquisition that comes from a good read-aloud.

The read-aloud offers wonderful opportunities for vocabulary growth; however, that benefit is only experienced if students are paying attention. Make sure that students are not losing the flow of the story by using TPTs to help students maintain comprehension. Pair-sharing is a simple and excellent way to process the story using higher-order thinking prompts. Certain stories lend themselves to wonderful higher-order discussions. Recently during family read-alouds of Cornelia Funke's book *The Thief Lord*, we became engaged in deep discussions. These included the possibilities of going backward or forward in time, the changes experienced by the characters, and the surprises that we didn't expect regarding the outcomes in the story. Each discussion required an analysis of what we had read and personal connections with what we have experienced. The read-aloud can lead to wonderful small-group or Pair-Share discussions that provide excellent opportunities for higher-order thinking.

TPTs like a Quick-Draw or a Chalkboard Splash (see Chapter 4) in response to a well-thought-out prompt or prediction-type question can also help students to analyze or consolidate what they've heard in the story. These can also provide you with a feel for how students are processing the story. Asking young students to demonstrate through their expressions how they would feel if they were the main character in a similar situation allows for teachers to see what students are comprehending. Follow-up explanations can be done in a quick Pair-Share.

Sometimes the very best TPT is simply looking up and capturing the mood of the story mirrored on the expressions of 25 young faces. When that happens, resist the urge to interrupt. The students' expressions themselves have just provided you with evidence of comprehension and emotional engagement. Anything else will just ruin the moment. The point that we hope to make here is this: the read-aloud is a very important part of a language-rich classroom. And if you're not sure that students are comprehending or are emotionally engaged in the story, then add a TPT. TPTs during the read-aloud can help students focus on what is being read and help them become engaged with the story.

Technology-Based TPTs

New technologies can present excellent opportunities to make sure that your students are cognitively engaged. In the following examples, we talk about two forms of technological applications that can result in participation and cognitive engagement by all of your students. Because the uses of each will need to be adapted to meet the particular context and resources of your teaching circumstance, we do not include the sections on How It Works, How to Ensure Higher-Order Thinking, and Pause to Apply. Instead, we ask you to consider each and talk them over with colleagues at your school to determine how each might enhance the learning opportunities for your students.

Classroom Clickers and Interactive Apps

One of the most popular high-participation technological tools that we have seen implemented in schools is the use of personal-response systems, or classroom clickers. With classroom clickers, selected-response items are posted on slides, and students each use a remote control to select what they feel is the right answer. Results are shown as a graph indicating the number of students that selected each item. Like clickers, digital apps have also been developed that allow students to use their cell phones to text in anonymous responses that will be displayed automatically on the screen. Other apps, like Kahoot (getkahoot.com), provide game-show-type experiences as a format for reviewing content. Clickers and personal response apps have their benefits, especially with regard to student participation, and they're definitely fun. But they are not a guaranteed home run. We have observed both effective and ineffective use of clickers. For example, in math, when students click and get the wrong answer, then what? When clickers were used well, we felt it was because the teacher felt free to detour from the slides. Even though clickers were usually used to review content already taught, teachable moments were still followed up with additional problems that were similar to the sample items on the slide, and the teacher circulated to make sure students understood the concepts. Effective use of clickers also included student interaction embedded within the presentations. "Ask your neighbor how he or she solved that problem." "Did you solve it in the same way?" "If you got the answer wrong, add a statement on your paper explaining why it was wrong." In many cases, wrong answers can be reviewed easily because clickers allow you to know how each student responded. Teachers tend to use clickers as an opportunity to answer questions with only one right answer. Instead, teachers need to also remind themselves to circulate and provide feedback and support to students who are struggling, and to take the time to focus on *why* answers are right and wrong.

Student teacher Heather Berrier used clickers in teaching 5th graders how our understanding of the Boston Massacre has been influenced by the voices in history to whom we gave the most credence. To help students understand the multiple points of view reflected in the retelling of this historical event, Berrier decided to present it multiple times. Students were first asked to examine an engraving drawn by Paul Revere, and they heard a quick description of the Boston Massacre. They were then asked to use electronic clickers to vote on who was most to blame for the Boston Massacre (the British, the Colonists, or both). A digital bar graph displayed the results of the vote. Students pair-shared their rationales, and then volunteers were selected to share their rationale with the class. Students then heard a historical account of the Boston Massacre from another perspective and were asked to vote again. At this point, many changed their vote. Again, they first voted individually, then interacted in pairs, and then volunteered responses, this time with a bit more enthusiasm, with more students wanting to volunteer. This procedure went on for four separate votes, some students vacillating each time, depending on the perspective given by each author. After each vote, students pair-shared, justifying their reason for the way they voted, and then volunteers shared with the class.

What was so striking about this lesson was that after each vote, more and more students began eagerly bouncing in their chairs, hands held high, passionately wanting an opportunity to express themselves and defend their choice before the whole class. Students had become invested in understanding this event and were more cognitively engaged than if they had simply read a chapter or passively listened to a presentation on the topic. At the end, Berrier gave all students an opportunity to explore and pair-share reasons for the multiple viewpoints and then portray their own viewpoint on an "engraving" done for all to see, in the form of a Chalkboard Splash (see Chapter 4). These students became emotionally engaged in the topic because of the ways that they were asked to process the information using Total Participation Techniques and higher-order thinking. Consider using clickers with questions that don't have easy answers followed up with opportunities for students to justify their responses. You will end up with fewer questions, but more interactions and more higher-order thinking.

Blogging

Consider the general concept behind blogging and online posts. These online journal formats have a great deal of potential when we look at them as an arena for academic collaboration. Though students may be asked to blog or write about a topic or prompt, they can also receive peer comments as feedback. Although there are certainly risks that would need to be carefully addressed, opportunities are also present for students to take ownership of their own learning. If every student is involved and the activity engages higher-order thinking, it has the potential to be a great tool for ensuring deeper learning.

Although online collaboration often requires an added investment of your time—at least until you get the hang of it—it offers a great opportunity for engaging students and keeping them accountable. We remember a conversation with a university student who admitted having never read a college textbook until her participation in an online assignment. The student admitted that in order to complete the required blogs and take part in the nested conversations, "I'm actually having to read the book." Depending on which provider your school uses or if you choose to host your individual site, access can be restricted to only those e-mail addresses that you approve. And, even if students select pseudonyms, as the teacher/site administrator, you may be able to see who is posting which comments. You can also set it up so that comments would need to receive your prior approval before actually being posted. Consider opening up a private account and trying it out using students' first names only (or pseudonyms). You may even want to use the Bounce Card (refer to Figure 6.4) as a way to support students in responding to each other. Our own child found them to be very helpful after being flustered by a middle school requirement that she respond to peers' weekly blog posts. We gave her a Bounce Card and found that she faithfully used it for weeks after she had been introduced to it.

Luehmann and MacBride (2009) examined how blogging was used in two high school classrooms (math and science). Although the two classrooms had different ways of structuring their use of blogs, these blogs allowed both teachers and students to share resources, post student responses to teacher prompts, hear student recordings of lesson highlights, and share student reflections on what was learned. One teacher credited the blogs with building a stronger community in her classroom and "breaking the ice" for the quieter students. One of the missed opportunities that the authors noted was the lack of student-led discussion. Students were clearly responding to the teacher, not each other. This shortcoming might be easily addressed by simply adding a requirement that students respond to a minimum number of peer posts (perhaps three). Students can also be assigned to lead discussions using an open-ended question. Teacher modeling can provide opportunities for students to practice how to phrase questions so that there are no easy answers.

8

TPT Wrap-Ups

Closure should lead to the students taking ownership of the learning. How are the students owning the learning? The teacher doesn't need to sum it up—the students need to sum it up. The students need to ask the questions that linger, and then those questions become a bridge to further learning.

Keely Potter, reading specialist

How you choose to end your lesson can make all the difference in whether or not students process and remember what was taught. One of the habits that we often fall into is not keeping track of the clock and ending a lesson whenever the allotted time ends. Instead, plan for less talk and more processing, so that you have enough time to adequately close your lesson in a way that provides you with evidence that students have learned your target content. In this chapter, we'll focus on ways to end lessons that provide you with evidence of what students learned, prior to their leaving the room.

IQ Cards (*Insight & Question*)

IQ Cards allow all students to share two things: an insight (I) and a question (Q). They also allow all students to read one another's insights and questions in a collaborative final step. Topics of study that often engage students' emotions and their intellect include units on historical conflicts and inequities, human responsibility, climate change, conservation, and controversial readings. These may very well be perfect fodder for a technique involving IQ Cards.

How It Works

1. Using an index card, ask students to record one new and important insight that they gained from the lesson (tell them to be as specific as possible) and one question that they have about the content (see Figure 8.1). Before they begin, let them know that others will be reading these cards, but will likely not know who wrote which *I* and *Q.* They should wait until the end of the activity to put their names on their cards.

Figure 8.1
IQ Card

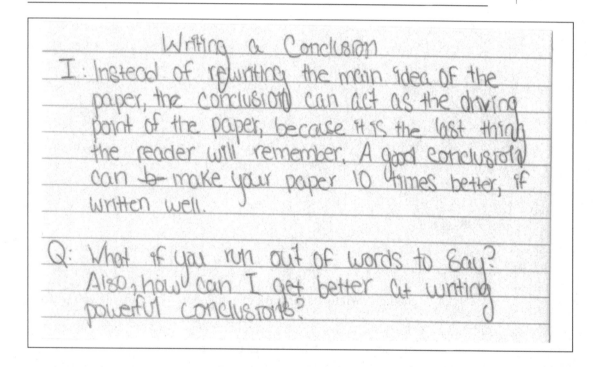

2. Ask students to take their card and stand in one large circle.
3. Without reading it, ask students to hand the card (facing up) to the person on their right. Do that about four times, so that the identities of the writers are a bit more obscured.
4. Once cards have been passed about four times, ask them to stop and read the card that they are holding in front of them.

5. Once they finish reading the card, ask them to pass it to the person on their right.

6. Tell them to keep reading and passing cards until they have their own card. Once they have their own card, they can stop and return to their seats and write their names on the backs of the cards.

7. Whole Group: Address commonalities in the insights and address the common questions that students had.

8. Ask students to put their names on their cards. Collect the cards, if you'd like to assess or monitor individual insights and questions.

How to Ensure Higher-Order Thinking

Rather than restating facts as their insights, ask students to think in terms of big-picture items. When you read the cards, make a special note of insights that were able to capture big-picture themes and revisit those during the whole-group time at the end, so that students have models of what big-picture items look like. You might say something like this: "Some of the big-picture insights that I recall reading touched on . . . ," along with an explanation as to what made them big-picture insights.

After they read their peers' cards, ask them to record two new insights and a new question on the backs of their cards. Review some or all and return them to the students soon after they've been collected.

Pause to Apply

The IQ Card technique allows you to capture the fleeting emotions linked to topics that are often not easy to assess, but that play an important role in helping your students understand other related topics. Take a look at the lessons that you have scheduled on the horizon. For which do you have difficult-to-test concepts that are measured by bigger-picture understandings? These would probably make great choices for your IQ Card wrap-up. In the example in Figure 8.1, a student reflects on the lesson's topic of writing a strong conclusion. Notice that her insight provides a specific detail about an aspect of writing a strong conclusion, rather than simply saying that a good conclusion is important. Because this lesson touched upon big-picture concepts that are easy to miss (but fundamental to good writing) the IQ Card closer allows the teacher an opportunity to assess that students are actually internalizing the big-picture concepts that are being presented, and it gives the teacher an opportunity to address common questions.

One-Word Summary

Matt Baker uses One-Word Summaries to allow his 8th grade students to summarize the essence of the content presented that day using just one word (Himmele, Himmele, & Potter, 2014). The students will often use a dry-erase marker to record their One-Word Summaries on their smooth desks. Baker circulates around the room asking for explanations or clarifications.

How It Works

1. Ask students to select one word that best describes the content presented that day, and record their word on Quick-Write sheets, in their notes, on dry-erase boards, or on their desks using dry-erase markers (as Matt Baker instructs his students).
2. Pair students using Appointment Agenda partners (see Chapter 6) or with peers seated close by. Ask them to explain their rationales for their one-word selections and to tell why the word is important enough to use as a One-Word Summary for the content learned. (Explanations can also be written on Quick-Write half sheets and submitted for teacher review.)
3. Ask students to, one at a time, call out their one-word response. Tell them that they can add a few words to clarify the connection if the connection is not clear.

How to Ensure Higher-Order Thinking

Use a Quick-Write half sheet to have students quickly explain their rationales for selecting the one word that they chose. If you are short on time, have them call out the one word and a quick sentence rationale.

Pause to Apply

This activity is versatile, brief, and can be used without much planning. What lesson are you teaching tomorrow or this week that would lend itself well to a One-Word Summary?

"What's It Really About?" Carousel

In Chapter 7, we introduced you to a Debate Team Carousel. In this chapter, we'd like to combine the format of a Debate Team Carousel with a "What's

It Really About?" Quick-Write (Himmele, Himmele, & Potter, 2014) that focuses on helping students get to the heart of analyzing themes and higher-order understandings related to the topic presented. Unlike the Debate Team Carousel presented earlier, this Carousel will only have three rounds.

How It Works

1. Ask students to respond to the first box (see Figure 8.2) by trying to dig deeply into the meaning behind the essence of what has been presented. They should not simply summarize what was taught, but they should look at the implications and the purposes behind the content. After students have responded to the first box, the teacher should signal the students to wrap up their responses and hand their papers to the person sitting to their right.

2. Each student should have a new paper in front of them. They should read their peer's response and respond to the question below their peer, by trying to dig deeper. "OK, but what's it *really, REALLY* about?" At the teacher's signal, students should wrap up their responses, write their name in the box, and pass the paper once more to their right.

3. At this point students should read their peers' responses and add any insights to the final box in the template, and add their names to the box. Papers should then be returned to their original owners.

4. Ask volunteers to share highlights. Collect the templates, so that you can read select samples in order to get a feel for the depth of student thinking.

How to Ensure Higher-Order Thinking

In *Total Literacy Techniques* (Himmele, Himmele, & Potter, 2014) we introduce the "What's It Really About?" Quick-Write. We describe how Keely Potter will often ask her students, "What's it about?" She'll follow that question up with the question, "Great, we talked about what it's about, but what's it *reeeeeally* about?" The exaggerated emphasis on the word *really* serves to alert the students that she is no longer seeking a literal response. At this point she wants students to dig deeper and get to the essence of the problem. In order to do that, students are being asked to analyze the deeper issues inherent in the topic. By getting students used to the "What's it really about?" question,

Figure 8.2

"What's It Really About?" Carousel

Name_____ Date_____

1. What's it *really* about?

2. OK, but what's it *really, REALLY* about?

_____ Responder's first name

3. Add anything else that might have been missed. Add to, or elaborate on, your peers' entries.

_____ Responder's first name

Source: Prompts from *Total Literacy Techniques: Tools to Help Students Analyze Literature and Informational Texts,* by Pérsida Himmele, William Himmele, and Keely Potter, 2014, Alexandria, VA: ASCD. Copyright 2014 by ASCD.

and by explaining the increased expectations that come along with that question, you'll be helping to ensure that students will be able to uncover the deeper meanings behind what is being taught.

Pause to Apply

As you review your curriculum, what would lend itself to allowing your students an opportunity to dig deeply into revisiting and processing the content in a way that uncovers deeper meanings? This activity is excellent for helping students analyze content that is rich with implications, inferences, and deeper purposes.

A Better Table Summary

This activity allows students to process the most essential elements of the day's lesson. They create a summary, combine summaries, and critically analyze their peers' summaries to come up with better summaries of the day's lesson.

How It Works

1. Ask every student to summarize the day's lesson using only one sentence.

2. Ask students to get into groups of no more than four and consolidate their sentence into one larger summary that contains all the essentials present in each of their sentences. Their new summary does not need to be contained in one sentence.

3. Give student groups one blank sheet of paper (preferably 8½" × 14" or 11" × 17") and one color marker (different color markers should be assigned to different tables). Ask them to fold the paper in three parts. Next, ask them to assign a scribe to record their table's summary using marker in the first folded section (caution them not to write too small).

4. Ask groups to pass their papers to a neighboring table. Each group should now have a summary that belongs to another table. Ask them to read it and to critically analyze what is missing. How can they improve this sentence summary so that it is more complete and includes elements that are essential to understanding the topic? Allow students to use notes. Ask them to write the improved sentence underneath the original sentence in the second folded section and to pass the paper to a different table (not the original table), that group should do the same in the third folded section.

5. Return the summaries to the original tables, and ask them to read and underline portions of the summaries that they think improved their original summaries.

6. Ask volunteers to share elements that improved the summaries.

How to Ensure Higher-Order Thinking

By its very nature, this activity requires that students critically analyze summaries to find ways to improve them and to make them more complete. To provide clear criteria for success, give students a specific number of improvements to make. For example, you might say, "Add two new concepts to improve the table summary."

Students may need assistance, so walk around and ask questions prompting them toward critical analysis. For example, you might say something like, "How did they address . . . ?" "Are there missing elements that can help clarify a potential misunderstanding with regard to . . . ?" For very incomplete summaries, pretend to completely misunderstand the summary, by taking it to a logical conclusion that is far off base. "So, you're saying that when combustion occurs, it's the result of someone turning on the lights?"

Pause to Apply

What are you teaching tomorrow or this week that would benefit from a final deeper review on the part of students? This is another versatile wrap-up that can be used on the spot as a way of asking students to wrap up their learning using the content that matters the most. As tables improve each other's sentence summaries, we often find them diligently referring to their books and notes to capture missing elements that the previous table forgot to add.

The Biggest *Aha* Quick-Write

The Biggest *Aha* Quick-Write allows you to capture what students feel are their most important insights learned from your lesson, and it does so in a format that requires only a few minutes of your class time.

How It Works

1. At the end of your lesson, ask students to think about and record their biggest *aha* on a Quick-Write half sheet, an index card, or a scrap piece of paper. (Biggest *aha* refers to their most important insight.)
2. Ask students to meet with someone they haven't spoken to in over a day and to share their *aha*.
3. Ask volunteers to share their *ahas* in a whole-group format.
4. Collect the cards and review them, or review a select few. Be sure to return the reflections even if you didn't get a chance to read them all. Let students know that you randomly selected a few to read.

How to Ensure Higher-Order Thinking

Ask the students to use specific details to explain why the *aha* was meaningful to them in their understanding of the content. For example, you might say, "Provide two examples of how your *aha* helps you better understand what you've learned today."

Pause to Apply

The Biggest *Aha* Quick-Write is a quick, versatile activity that can provide closure to almost any lesson. Student *ahas* can be very enlightening in terms of knowing what was important to them. You may be surprised that students grasp concepts that you had not clearly spelled out for them, or that you hadn't intentionally emphasized.

The Biggest *Aha* Bar Graph

The Biggest *Aha* Bar Graph allows you to capture what students feel are their most important insights learned and see commonalities among them. Basically, it's a bar graph constructed using your students' biggest *ahas*. It allows you to peek into their minds as a group and see what portions of your lesson made the biggest impact on students and what needs further attention. It also provides an opportunity to review the deeper concepts for those students who are still processing the content at a superficial level of understanding.

How It Works

1. At the end of your lesson, ask students to think about and record their biggest *ahas* on a Quick-Write half sheet, index card, or precut pieces of paper. (It's important that all papers be the same size, to make sure that students aren't using scrap paper or varying sizes of notebook paper.)
2. Begin by asking one volunteer to share his or her biggest *aha*.
3. Ask the same student to bring a sheet of paper to a designated area in the room, grab a piece of tape, and tape it to the wall, door, board, bulletin board, or wherever you'd like to have the Biggest *Aha* Bar Graph posted.

4. Ask peers who selected the same or a similar *aha* to stand up, line up next to the bar graph, and read theirs aloud. After reading it, they should tape it above the other students' papers, forming the first bar graph column. Occasionally, students will share different *ahas* that may merit their own column. When this happens, validate their responses and ask them to form a new category by taping it next to (not above) the original response. Go back to the earlier category to finish constructing the column, before moving to the new category.

5. Ask a student who has not posted a paper on the graph to share what his or her biggest *aha* was. Repeat the procedure, by asking students with a similar *aha* to read theirs and come up and post them.

6. By the end of this activity, you should have a bar graph made of student comment cards, with each of the categories representing similar comments. You can quickly grasp which concepts made the biggest impact, and you can tell if others need to be revisited. Again, make sure that students write their *ahas* on the same type or size of paper, so that the bar graph isn't skewed.

How to Ensure Higher-Order Thinking

We have found this activity to be very helpful in gauging for the depth of understanding that students walk away with. Often students will have a very literal understanding of what was taught, and it is clear that they only acquired a surface-level knowledge of the concepts being introduced. This activity helps teachers to know that, so they can continue emphasizing those essential concepts that are important to digging deeper in the lesson. Remind the students to choose a big-picture item, rather than an obscure fact. Highlight those that chose big-picture items by pointing out how they help us as learners to understand the root of the problem, issue, or concept.

Pause to Apply

This activity sounds as though it will take a long time, but it rarely does. Usually we find that we end up with four or five total categories. If you are short on time, only ask the students who introduce a new category to read their responses. Ask those with like responses to grab a piece of tape and place it in bar graph format. We typically precut strips of tape and have them dangling from a desk, so that students can quickly grab a piece of tape and use it to attach their response. You can also have several tape dispensers available to make the process run more smoothly.

The Three-Sentence Wrap-Up

In giving university exams, we have learned the hard way about the need for specifying a word limit on constructed-response items. When students knew the content, the responses were direct and clearly addressed the topic. When students did not have a clear understanding of the content, they would often add everything under the sun that was even remotely related to the question in hope of getting some credit. Somewhere embedded in the lengthy response was the correct answer, but we suspected that the student had little idea as to which part it was. When we started adding approximate word limits (no more than 20 words, for example), students had to be selective. They were forced to directly address the question and not stray from the topic.

By asking for Three-Sentence Wrap-Ups, you eliminate the tendency to add every peripheral item discussed. Students have to be selective, determine what is most important, and then succinctly sum it up. Having to summarize something lengthy, in three sentences or fewer, can be a bit of a challenge. But it requires that students sift out what is important and sum up their understandings in a concise way.

How It Works

1. At the end of a unit, have students summarize it in three sentences or fewer.
2. Have small groups get together to share and refine their summaries.

How to Ensure Higher-Order Thinking

Ask students to get into small groups and compare their Three-Sentence Wrap-Ups. Is there a way to pare the summary down to even fewer sentences and fewer words? What parts are essential? This additional activity will require that students further analyze what they have selected and determine what is most important. Finish this off with a Chalkboard Splash (see Chapter 4), with the small groups writing their final wrap-up sentence (or sentences) on the board.

After individuals meet with their small groups, you can also ask students to add a fourth sentence that addresses the topic's relevance toward life. The fourth sentence might begin with "This is important because . . . ."

Pause to Apply

This is a simple on-the-spot activity that can really go far in allowing students to wade through the lesson's content and repackage it in a very brief form. Although many of the activities presented in this book are simple to use, they can easily be forgotten in the urgency to cover content. A simple way to remember to use this activity is to post the directions in the back of the room or in a place where you can easily see them. You can do the same for any of the activities in this chapter that can be implemented on the spot. By having these directions posted, you can refer to them during your planning and during your lesson.

A–Z Sentence Summary

At the end of her lesson on Civil War weaponry, 8th grade history teacher Liz Lubeskie gave students a letter from a cardboard cut-out alphabet. She then asked them to create a "sentence summary" that began with the letter she had given them. Here are a few examples of what the students created:

> **J** = Just in time for the Civil War, weapons were enhanced by great accuracy and distance.
> **V** = Very fast firing of weapons caused many casualties during the Civil War.
> **Y** = Young men were drafted into the war and used guns like rifles and the Gatling gun.

Lubeskie also uses alphabet refrigerator magnets to create a Chalkboard Splash review. At the end of a lesson, students choose magnetic letters, attach these to the whiteboard, and write their sentence summaries on the board. This activity is a great wrap-up to almost any lesson, enabling students to share and contribute to a larger-scale whole-class summary.

How It Works

1. At the end of a teacher-led content presentation, assign students a letter of the alphabet (or give them a cardboard or magnetic letter).

2. Ask students to create a one-sentence summary of the presentation, beginning their sentence with the assigned letter.

3. Do a Chalkboard Splash, attaching the sentence and magnetic letter to the board so students can review their peers' sentence summaries.

4. Before ending the lesson, call out the letters sequentially from A to Z to cue students to read their sentences out loud.

Word to the wise: Here's a bit of advice that we learned the hard way. Don't comment on how excellent a response might be, no matter how tempted you are to linger on a response, or you'll find yourself trying to imitate that same enthusiasm across 26 letters. Instead, simply say, "Thank you," and then call out the next letter.

How to Ensure Higher-Order Thinking

One way to ensure higher-order thinking with this activity is to ask students to add a relevance component to their sentences. For example, students can create a second sentence to their A–Z Sentence Summary by completing the sentence starter "This is important because . . ." or "This affects us today because . . . ." This relevance piece can be added to a sentence summary in any content area. If students are learning about different kinds of soil, for example, it's also important that they know why that information is worth knowing. What are the implications of various soils for the different vegetation, wildlife, or even building materials in the area in which they live?

Pause to Apply

A–Z Sentence Summaries are a wonderful on-the-spot wrap-up activity, and the colorful magnets or cardboard letters add a little spice to it. Finishing it with a Chalkboard Splash rather than a simple Pair-Share allows you to see at once what everybody learned. Another added benefit of this activity is that it will fit with almost anything that is being taught in almost any content area. For example, what did you teach yesterday? How might the students' creation of A–Z Sentence Summaries have helped you with the wrap-up portion of that lesson?

1, 2, 3 O'Clock

This wrap-up technique allows you to quickly review three important questions by having students respond to and discuss them with a designated classmate. It can be modified to include more or fewer questions, depending on the amount of time you have.

How It Works

1. Select three questions that are fundamental to understanding the concepts being taught.
2. Type them on a PowerPoint slide, or print them on half sheets (see Figure 8.3).
3. Give students a few minutes to provide a written response to the three questions.
4. Ask them to meet with their 1:00 appointment (see Appointment Agendas in Figure 6.3), and respond to the question reserved for 1:00. Both partners should share. Students can modify or "borrow" ideas from their partners and add them to their responses.
5. Ring a bell, and ask partners to meet with their 2:00 appointments and share the designated response. Repeat for the 3:00 question.
6. Ask volunteers to share their thoughts. Clarify any misunderstandings.

How to Ensure Higher-Order Thinking

Ask students to collect one or two insights that they will borrow from their classmates. Ask them to take a pen or pencil to their appointment so that they can capture ideas and label them as "new insights." Use big questions that ask for implications or that require mastery of the surface knowledge, but that use content in a way that demonstrates that students understand the big picture of what is being discussed.

Pause to Apply

This technique fits almost any lesson. Think about the next lesson that you will be teaching today or tomorrow. What three open-ended questions could you ask in a 1, 2, 3 O'Clock format? This simple closer can go a long way in supporting student understanding, primarily because it involves processing the content alongside others.

For a follow-up session, consider opening up the lesson with a review of these 1, 2, 3 O'Clock entries, except that for the review, alter it so that they are meeting with their 4:00, 5:00, and 6:00 appointments. This way, students will be exposed to a variety of perspectives on these very important questions, and you're able to start off at the exact point where you ended.

Figure 8.3
1, 2, 3 O'Clock

1, 2, 3 O'Clock
1:00: In what ways were the presidencies of Theodore Roosevelt and FDR different?
2:00: Describe the impact that Theodore Roosevelt's foreign policy had on how the U.S. was viewed by other countries.
3:00: Describe the impact that FDR's foreign policy had on how the U.S. was viewed by other countries.

List, Group, Label (*End of Unit Review*)

List, Group, Label is a technique developed by Hilda Taba (1967). It is an excellent way to have students collaboratively "spill their brains" onto a sheet of paper at the end of a multi-lesson unit. We've modified it here so that it embeds the first step of the Ripple, by asking students to brainstorm on their own first. We have seen this activity successfully done with 2nd grade through college-age students. In fact, we frequently use this activity with our undergraduate and graduate students to either begin or close a unit.

How It Works

1. **Individual Brainstorm:** Using the main topic of study, ask students to individually brainstorm and record all the concepts associated with the main topic. Give the students two to three minutes to jot down some thoughts. For example, your topic might be "Landforms."
2. **Group Brainstorm:** Place students in groups of no more than four. Give each group a piece of chart paper, or an 11" × 17" or 8½" ×

14" sheet of paper. (It should be large enough so that they can all see it when they later hold it up to share it with other groups.) Ask the groups to select a scribe to record the group's contributions on the paper. They should begin by writing the topic in large print in the center of the paper. The scribe uses only one color marker to write the concepts that group members share. Although students will be using their individually brainstormed lists, they should also freely add to the list as new ideas pop up. They should shoot for as many concepts as possible.

3. **Making Categories:** During this next step, the students will need several different colors of markers. Ask students to review the contributions, begin making categories, and assign each category a color. For example, students might notice that, for a concept map of World War II, the concepts of Germany, Japan, and Italy all fit under the category "Axis Powers." They should circle or underline each concept using the color that was assigned to that group. Ask students to make a legend (or key), so that others can identify the category by looking at the color.

4. **Share your List, Group, Label:** As groups finish creating their List, Group, Label charts, ask them to share their chart with other tables who are also finished.

5. **Whole Group:** Display the charts and ask for volunteers to share commonalities noticed and any surprises or forgotten items in their charts.

How to Ensure Higher-Order Thinking

After students have shared with another group, ask them to quickly add any forgotten items that they picked up from their peers to their charts. You may also want to have groups use a pen or pencil so that the concepts are distinguishable from those that they thought of on their own. Let them know that you're only asking them to use a different writing tool because you want to get a feel for how much they are learning from each other.

Pause to Apply

Think about the units that you'll be teaching this year. Which units will require a great deal of concepts? How might you use List, Group, Label to wrap up an intense unit of study and allow students to review major concepts in a novel way?

As you circulate around the room, try not only to focus on what students have written on the larger chart, but also get a feel for what students shared on their individual charts.

The Six-Slide Review (*End-of-Unit Review*)

The Six-Slide Review asks students to design the layout for a presentation with six PowerPoint slides that capture the most important aspects of what was learned throughout a multi-lesson unit. Groups then get together to consolidate their slides into a final design. In a final Chalkboard Splash, students individually share their most important slide. (Note: This technique does not use actual PowerPoint slides, but instead uses a paper template for planning a PowerPoint presentation. If students have access to the technology, it can also be modified to make use of actual PowerPoint slides.)

How It Works

1. Give each student a six-slide template (see Figure 8.4). Ask them to look through their notes and materials and selectively capture the highlights of what was learned using pictures and statements on six slides. Rather than using captions, their statements should include clear, complete thoughts that provide evidence that they understand the most important aspects of the unit.

2. Place students in groups of no more than four to share their slides. Using chart paper or 11" × 17" size paper, ask them to sketch the layout for a Six-Slide Review that captures what was most important from their individual slide template. Ask them to be selective.

3. When they are finished, each group should present their design to another group.

4. As a final wrap-up, ask students to do a Chalkboard Splash by drawing the one slide that they feel was the most important to them. They don't have to agree. Ask them to add an explanation within or next to the slide. (If you'd like to collect and review these, the final slide can be drawn on a half sheet of paper and placed on the chalk tray or taped around the room. If the students use paper, ask them to do a Gallery Walk, so that they can see one another's slides.)

Figure 8.4
The Six-Slide Review Template

Name		Topic

How to Ensure Higher-Order Thinking

Before students share with one another, let them know that they will be asked to add two or three new insights to the backs of their individually created slide shows. This will ensure that they listen to each other, honor one another's contributions, and add to their own learning.

Pause to Apply

This activity works well when there is a great deal of content to review. We've labeled this an end-of-unit review because it is time consuming. The first step, when students create individual templates of the six slides, may take them 10 minutes because it requires students to refer to any readings and notes that they have. As they are creating their slideshows, circulate and review their materials to see what they've grasped and to assess who may need additional support.

Section 3:

TPTs in More Depth

9

TPTs as Formative Assessment Tools

TPTs make great formative assessments. The students leave your class and you know exactly where to pick up the next day, instead of wondering if you need to review the concept with the whole class or pull a select group of kids. You have this great information, so it makes your planning so much easier.

Shannon Paules, 7th and 8th grade English teacher

The best kinds of assessments are formative in nature. The purpose for collecting information from this type of assessment is to ultimately improve learning. Formative assessments help teachers evaluate students' knowledge and understanding and then adjust their teaching to produce improved student learning (Black & Wiliam, 1998). Formative assessments do not simply inform teaching; they actually result in the *formation* of new learning. In contrast to a summative assessment, the results of which only sum up what was learned, formative assessments actually cause new learning to take shape.

According to Nichols, Meyers, and Burling (2009), an assessment qualifies as being called formative "if the instruction results in increased positive outcomes relative to the expected outcome if no changes had been made" (pp. 22–23). In their framework, the authors set forth guidelines for evaluating whether a formative assessment is, in fact, formative. Their framework eventually ends up asking the following question: "Does information from the assessment lead to changes that improve achievement?" (p. 16). Formative assessments can have powerful positive results on student learning because teacher behavior becomes informed and instruction becomes targeted toward specific needs. At its finest, formative assessment engages students in taking ownership of their own learning and in their own self-improvement.

In the process of gathering information on the status of their students' learning, teachers rely on their professional expertise on a day-to-day, hour-by-hour, minute-by-minute basis to determine the emerging needs of their students. When we refer to using formative assessment, we are referring to the informed judgments that the teacher strategically gathers and uses within the classroom to move a student from point A to point B. Such assessment requires skilled teachers who continuously take note of and respond to where their students are. Formative assessment is a response to what students need, and effective use results in student progress. As contrasted with summative assessment, which captures the end of learning (e.g., from an end-of-unit test), formative assessment requires that teachers constantly assess and respond to the feedback during these assessments while they are teaching. Used consistently, TPTs can function as formative assessments by affecting learning, providing teachers with ongoing data about what students understand and what they need.

How TPTs Can Change Your Expectations

TPTs are powerful in that they can change the way you teach and what you expect from your students. According to 6th grade teacher Meghan Babcock, TPTs have altered not only her students' performance but also her own expectations as a co-teacher. "There are times where we'll stop and think, 'I'm so surprised that the student said that.' But we would never know what the student was thinking unless we were doing activities that required that the whole class participate. And it's changed the way that I ask questions because I realize that they can do it." For Babcock, TPTs have provided valuable information regarding students' capabilities, resulting in her offering them more challenging learning opportunities. Babcock went deeper, providing more targeted prompts that pushed her students to higher-order thinking because of the new knowledge she gained through her use of TPTs as formative assessment. She explains:

> Deliberately using TPTs has made me more effective. And it gives the kids a more even playing field. . . . I think I thought I was doing this on a normal basis, but it wasn't until I actually assessed my planning that I became more deliberate. It's helped make me a more effective teacher, getting every kid to respond, and thinking about when to do this . . . when you make it more deliberate, the kids really rise.

Chalkboard Splashes and Hold-Ups in Formative Assessment

Chalkboard Splashes and Hold-Ups offer great opportunities for formative assessment at almost any age. Chalkboard Splashes, for example, provide an excellent opportunity for us to debrief and assess students' understandings of an assigned reading in our graduate and undergraduate classes on assessment. On the due date of a highly technical reading on gathering validity-related evidence, we assign three sections of the whiteboards to three different forms of validity evidence, and one section to the relevance question "So what? Why should I care?" Students are first given a brief think time to explain each form of validity in their own words at their seats. They then walk up to the whiteboards and in the various sections jot down their understandings of each form. Invariably, the concept of *construct-related evidence of validity* seems to stump many students. This is apparent by statements that begin with things like "I think it means . . ." and "This one is really confusing . . . ." As students step back and consolidate their peers' statements by analyzing similarities, differences, and surprises, the activity gives each student a better grasp of what the terms mean and why they are important. And the activity gives us a starting point for understanding what specific pieces of the concepts confused them and what pieces of relevance need to be brought out.

We review the various concepts through a Hold-Up in which the three different forms of validity evidence are assigned a card, and a fourth card says *None of the Above* (usually this card is held up for examples that describe evidence of reliability rather than validity). In the Hold-Up, students work collaboratively, sharpening one another's understandings of the concepts before voting. Through the interaction inherent in the Hold-Up, students learn from one another. And we get a good feel for how well students understand the concepts by reshaping questions to address shaky understandings and allowing students to justify their responses to their peers, and retaking votes when necessary. We then end the class with the same Chalkboard Splash, but this time students' explanations have been sharpened by interactions with peers, real-life examples, and their being able to self-assess and pinpoint exactly where their understanding was faulty. The final Chalkboard Splash lets us know if we can move on to the next topic or if we need to backtrack and revisit specific concepts.

The focus on the formation of learning is important. Had we done a Chalkboard Splash and not allowed time for students to consolidate their peers' thoughts and to look for similarities, differences, and surprises, or had we not reshaped questions along the way and allowed for peer interaction during Hold-Ups, the assessments may have gone nowhere. The Chalkboard Splash may not have resulted in the formation of learning, but it may have served to provide us with a picture of what students did or did not understand. However, formative assessments are powerful in that they should not only provide you with a picture of what students know, but also allow you to affect and further develop what students know by specifically targeting what they need.

In another example, 5th grade teacher Courtney Cislo explains how she uses Whiteboard Hold-Ups to frequently monitor students' understanding of math concepts:

> You have a quick assessment that is really good for letting your lesson flow in the way that the students need it to. Right on the spot you know, because you can see that they're all forgetting to put a zero as a place holder. And you think to yourself, "Do I need to go back and reteach this?"

Reading Your Students

For reading specialist Keely Potter, formative assessments "allow me to assess who is staying in the literal, and who's moving toward making inferences and using symbolism and understanding the concepts more deeply." By reviewing student journal entries, she was able to decide whom to focus on during individual students' analysis of text. The information obtained allowed her to strategically visit certain students during their Quick-Write times. She explains:

> The thing I love about the open-ended Quick-Write is that on one end, you can find your evidence of the literal, but you also see evidence of your own teaching, and you also get evidence of the personal celebrations that kids share. For example, this student is really starting to believe in herself, in her ability to connect to symbolism. She's becoming competent in her analytical abilities and to know where she was and how far she has come. Quick-Writes allow you to get inside their heads.

Eighth grade English teacher Matt Baker echoed these sentiments: "Quick-Writes are fantastic. You get an awful lot of information from a kid just from three minutes' worth of 'This is what I did today,' and 'This is what

happened to me,' and 'This is where I was frustrated and I fixed it this way.'"
Baker was consistent in reading and responding to the Quick-Writes. His
students' metacognitive Quick-Writes were kept in one place, with what they
had written the previous day preceding what they wrote today. This simple
organizational setup enabled Baker to quickly refer to reflections recorded in
sequence a day or even days earlier.

The One-Liner Wall

Potter used a One-Liner Wall to highlight statements that students had written
in their reading packets. A One-Liner Wall is composed of selected students'
statements from their writings. The selected sentences are either copied onto
sentence strips and affixed to a designated wall (titled the One-Liner Wall),
or copied onto a piece of chart paper that captures a certain theme. Each line
is accompanied with a byline that identifies the student who wrote it. Potter
says, "I love to find the one-liners and pull them out and highlight them on the
One-Liner Wall, because they lead you to a theme. Where is the theme leading
us? The One-Liner Wall allows you to bring it to a shared experience."

Potter uses the one-liners as formative assessments and he uses them to
guide students to more symbolic thinking. According to Potter,

> It allows the students to see each other's work, to talk about it, so
> that if they don't have the ideas in their own heads, they're getting
> it from each other. Capturing these kinds of ideas and putting these
> up in the form of one-liners becomes a scaffold for the others at
> the same time. . . . For example, here's a student whose writing
> is really structured. She's not where everyone else is. She's in the
> literal. So I pulled out select phrases that should be validated.
> You could differentiate for this student who hasn't developed
> complete thoughts, by selecting words and phrases that should be
> validated, that model the symbolism even briefly. What it does is, it
> encourages her to do more of it.

The One-Liner Wall evolved from Potter's experience in an urban setting
in a school with a high percentage of students with diverse learning and
linguistic needs. "With those that could not produce a complete work, it was
wonderful to find pieces of their work and validate their journey. . . . It was like
the wall where everybody was welcome."

TPTs and Student Grades

If we see the purpose for assigning grades as an attempt to accurately portray a student's status on a continuum of learning, then it makes sense to include what we discover through Total Participation Techniques in student grading. Anecdotal records taken during and shortly after the TPTs are assessments that are just as important as end-of-unit tests. In fact, they can offer greater reliability (because of students' repeat performances on several tasks aimed at measuring the same conceptual understandings) and more opportunities for making valid inferences (because teachers have a more accurate picture of what students know).

Keep records of student progress on a checklist that has each of your students' names along with enough space to jot down notes regarding individual progress or concerns. Add just a few notes per lesson, perhaps with a goal of recording at least one note per student for any given week. Collect and read Quick-Writes whenever possible. And photocopy Quick-Writes that you believe provide an accurate reading of what the child understands. Place these in your students' portfolios. Record notes regarding participation and concept development. Be systematic in collecting work in portfolios that will give you ongoing maps of the students' progress. And move away from the idea that student grades should be solely dependent on a few tests and assignments. Then, when you get a test score that appears to be an outlier (which may happen more often for English language learners and students with special needs than others), you'll be better able to determine whether the test was or was not actually measuring what you hoped it would be measuring. For example, it is common for tests aimed at measuring mathematical problem solving to actually be measuring linguistic proficiency and reading comprehension. When you get a test score that does not fit with the inferences that you've obtained from your formative assessments, it should raise red flags and cause you to further investigate what the student has actually learned. But you'll only know this if you've been using formative assessment in the classroom.

Reflection Questions

- Think about how you may have used TPTs this week. Were there missed opportunities for the formation of learning? If so, what might you do to address this the next time you assign that particular activity?

- What kinds of TPTs can operate as formative assessment tools that can enhance teaching and learning in your classroom?
- Are you making the most of formative assessments? Are you keeping records of what you discover through the assessments and using them to affect student learning? If not, what simple steps could you implement tomorrow that will help you do this?

10

Building a TPT-Conducive Classroom

We blended the groups heterogeneously, and all of the students that we didn't expect to see rise were some of the top thinkers, and they were contributing and participating in ways that we never would have known they could, had we not used Total Participation Techniques.

Meghan Babcock, 6th grade teacher

Building a TPT-conducive classroom requires intentionality. For TPTs to run smoothly, teachers must establish a classroom culture conducive to student interaction and to students taking on active roles in the classroom learning community. Teachers have to get comfortable with losing some of the control they have over talk time and over wide but shallow coverage of a huge amount of content. This shift in approach doesn't come naturally to most people. Think about it. If students are talking more, that means teachers are talking less. Teachers also have to create classroom communities that honor student differences and promote peer acceptance, where students feel confident to share, and where trust abounds. The environment must be one in which teachers trust students, students trust teachers, students trust one another, and students trust themselves. Sixth grader Sara expressed the need to trust herself when she said, "I learned that you have to trust what you are doing because anything could be right. I also became more observant. . . . We would stop and think, why is the author saying this?" Students who get to this point become more confident and more likely to contribute to the learning that is happening in the classroom.

Creating a TPT-conducive classroom also requires consistency and follow-through. It requires the shaping of opportunities so that students will shine—and even surprise themselves in the process. The TPT-conducive classroom thrives on student differences and the collectively bigger way of looking at things that these differences provide. It allows all students to flourish and think deeply.

The best thing about implementing TPTs is that teaching is no longer a guessing game as to who is experiencing growth. With TPTs, you get to observe growth as it happens. You get to celebrate the learning right alongside your students.

Appreciating Student Differences

We can learn a great deal about appreciation for differences from the business world. Global markets expert Maria Bartiromo described how Jack Welch, former CEO of General Electric, brought out the best in people: "One of the reasons I appreciated Jack Welch so much when he was running GE was that he let us know that individual creativity thrilled him" (2010, p. 49). In describing how he was able to get the very best from his workers, Bartiromo writes that Welch described himself as an orchestra leader. Not all of the instruments are the same. "The leader's job is to touch every one of those people so they know they're free to think and do things better" (p. 49).

Are our students free to think and do things better? How would our students react to knowing that they are all unique and that their differences are not just tolerated, but that their differences, perspectives, and diverse experiences actually add to the small-group and classroom learning experiences? What would our classrooms look like if we truly believed that of our students? This type of mentality has the potential to change our classrooms.

We witnessed this appreciation for student differences during the interactions in Keely Potter and Meghan Babcock's class. During one particular Quick-Draw activity, reading specialist Potter was walking around the room, periodically pausing to comment on students' illustrations. She stopped to reflect on one student's Quick-Draw. After the student explained her use of symbolism in the drawing, Potter probed. "Do other teachers know that you're this deep?" The student responded, "No, I don't think so." We talked to Potter afterward regarding the conversation, and her response was as notable as it was depressing:

She hasn't had the opportunities to show what she knows. She doesn't get to show what she knows verbally or in writing. She never shares in class. Never. Ever. I've witnessed that firsthand. It's easy to miss all that she has. She is a perfect example of a kid who is going to be completely overlooked without the use of TPTs. She's got this creative, abstract way of thinking, but no one will ever know that because of her silence.

Let's make a commitment to ourselves and to our students that we will not be the type of teacher who never knows how deep our students' thinking can be. Let's instead use multiple ways of giving students opportunities to demonstrate the depths of their cognitive abilities.

Fostering Student Collaboration

Fifth grade teacher Courtney Cislo believes that "nothing is more valuable than students talking to each other. These kids are so smart; they have great ideas. It's important for them to share and hear each other's ideas and not just mine." During our observations in TPT-conducive classrooms, we worked with teachers who shared Cislo's sentiment. Each valued the role of interaction, expressing the importance of students working in groups and learning from each other.

Although we consistently found students working in mixed groups, the teachers expressed different views about how to group students. Seventh and 8th grade English teacher Shannon Paules and 8th grade English teacher Matt Baker believe that when students select their own groups, they are more willing to collaborate and share with each other. Their trust in student choice was also evident in other areas of their teaching and fit well with their priorities. They had constant interaction but allowed students to demonstrate responsibility by selecting groups with whom they could work best. Paules also had her students' desks deliberately arranged in U-shaped groups of four, so that she could walk right in the middle of the group and interact with them. Courtney Cislo used a variety of methods for grouping, including allowing students to choose their own groups, grouping students strategically, and grouping students heterogeneously. Her choice of how to group students was determined by the activity that she was doing. Mike Pyle grouped students strategically according to not only academic strengths but also social skills. He used the terms "face buddy" when he wanted students to work heterogeneously in a certain pairing combination with the person across from them, and "shoulder buddy" when he wanted students to work heterogeneously using a different pairing priority with the person sitting next to them. Student seating arrangements had been predetermined. His pairing of students was also determined by the activity.

Regardless of the way students were grouped within these classrooms, it was the teacher's informed judgments that made each grouping scenario work. Teachers had made decisions based on their own teaching styles and on their experiences with the students in their classrooms. They had also made decisions based on the trust that they placed in each student, believing that, although the students were different, each had valuable gifts to share within their groups.

Peer Rejection and Peer Acceptance

As delightful as children can be, they can also be a bit of a challenge—especially in their treatment of each other. Part of our job is to create an environment where students feel safe to participate and that allows all students to shine and display their unique talents to their peers. The degree to which children participate is closely linked with self-concept. Not surprisingly, those who participate more have a higher self-concept (Dykman & Reis, 1979). In a study of 398 children, peer rejection had a direct connection to class participation. When peer rejection ceased, participation increased (Ladd, Herald-Brown, & Reiser, 2008).

It's no surprise that nonparticipatory students tend to seat themselves on the periphery, where they can best hide in safety. "By distancing themselves in seats that reduce the probability of inclusion, students minimize the risk of self-deprecating experiences" (Dykman & Reis, 1979, p. 352). So, how do we create classrooms where everyone feels free to participate? For the answer to that question, we'd like to refer you to Chapter 2, where we introduce the concept of "rippling" your questions and prompts. When you ripple your prompts, you ease students into the discussion. Because they must first respond individually, you give them time to think through their response, and then have them share it in pairs or small groups—a low-risk situation—before asking for volunteers in a whole-group setting.

Building Confidence

Often the risk of peer rejection supersedes the importance of participation. That's where teachers come in. Courtney Cislo takes a proactive approach to encouraging participation from those who have experienced a lack of academic success:

> It's so rewarding to see the excitement build in a typically low-performing student once I've validated his or her answer. All it takes is going up to a group and listening in on their conversation and making a quick little comment like, "Wow, I love how you used details from the book to support your answer. I hope you share that." Then when it comes time for the traditional Q & A, those students are some of the first ones to have their hands in the air.

English teacher Shannon Paules also noted the confidence that TPTs provide for students. "It gives them confidence . . . because they think to themselves, 'I know I'm on the right track, and when the teacher calls on me, I'm going to be able to answer, and I'm not going to look stupid in front of my friends.'"

Cislo notices that in her classroom, encouraging those who have experienced peer rejection pays off in terms of overall increased participation:

> I can think of kids that never participated at the beginning of the year, but that has changed. Now the majority of the students are being validated by their peers, which leaves the remaining students to be validated by me. For those students, I make it a point to stop by their desks and say, "Wow, that is creative," or "You made an interesting point. Good thinking!" There are even times when I'll point out what students wrote during a [Chalkboard Splash] and say, "This statement reminds me of . . ." or "I wonder who wrote that."

Cislo believes that teachers play a key role in supporting students in being accepted by their peers:

> With the students who are not popular, they used to participate the least . . . before I validated them. If I go over and say, "Oh, I love that answer. I hope that you can feel free to share that with the class," they end up sharing more often. The encouragement needs to come from somewhere, either from peers or from me. If they are

encouraged and validated, they will be more likely to participate. But the teacher has a responsibility of modeling social skills, too. You have to model that acceptance, too.

Eighth grade history teacher Liz Lubeskie voiced a similar opinion. She has a walking club that meets and walks during school club times at the end of the day. When she notices that a student is struggling to fit in or needs someone to talk to, she'll invite that student to join her for walking club. Her popularity as a teacher, and the fact that she acknowledges the gifts a student has, supports a student's acceptance among his or her peers.

From preschool through high school, teachers can play a critical role in supporting students who struggle socially. Often students' awkwardness is a result of repeatedly experiencing peer rejection. For these students, saying anything in class or elsewhere takes extra effort and becomes a risk. Teachers can be proactive in supporting these students by demonstrating acceptance and strategically planning their successful inclusion in academic and social activities throughout the day.

Student confidence also comes from experiencing academic success. Meghan Babcock used to exclusively teach a learning support class (made up of students with mild disabilities). She now collaborates with teachers in teaching mixed 6th grade groups. Reflecting on the progress of the students with special needs, she noted the following:

> By the time I get them in 6th grade, I feel like they're all shut down; they don't even want to try anymore. I feel like there's such a learned feeling of failure that they don't want to try. It takes away all intrinsic motivation. But there's just so much worth in these little [TPT] structures. It's making them feel smart.

Potter continued, "Students were allowed to express themselves through the use of TPTs. They had so much to say and they didn't even know it." Her comments express the power of a well-placed prompt—and a participation requirement—hidden within a fun activity. The TPTs have the potential to build student confidence as well as student learning.

Building Trust: The Teacher's Belief System

Building an environment based on trust comes easier to some teachers than to others. Generally speaking, teachers who gain trust easily use body language that tells students that they care about what everyone has to say. These teachers even send a clear message that they like each student. Engaging with these teachers involves very little risk. But building trust is an uphill battle for others who are sarcastic or overly critical, and who use people's names in illustrations of what not to do, as examples to get their point across. At some point students figure out that they'll be the next victim of sarcasm, criticism, or the illustration of what not to do. Engaging with these teachers involves a bit more risk. Most teachers behave somewhere in between. They have overcrowded curricula that need to get covered, pacing guides with which they are not keeping pace, and a bunch of kids getting in the way. Perhaps they care deeply about their students, but somehow that message has gotten lost in the mad rush to cover curricula and get students test-ready by springtime.

Trust is essential for a TPT-conducive environment. Students are being asked to take risks, and they need to know that what they say will be valued. Trust takes work. It is earned. And your students need to know that they can trust you. So slow down and analyze. What have you done today to build trust? What can you do tomorrow to build trust?

According to Potter, "This is about the teacher's belief system. Do teachers really believe that kids are capable of big things? Even the poor kids, or the Title I kids, or the Learning Support kids?" As Potter suggests, in addition to trusting you, your students need to know that you trust them. Do you trust them? Do you trust that they want to learn? Do you trust that they have amazing things to share? Do you trust that they can learn from one another, especially *because* of their learning differences? Do you trust that if they trust themselves, amazing things will happen? If not, establishing trust will be a journey for both you and your students, because if you are asking your students to demonstrate active participation and cognitive engagement, they'll need to know that you trust them. So work on convincing yourself. Post the following statements in a place where you can see them every day, and during classroom lulls, read and revisit the statements. (See Appendix B for a reproducible version.) Then go ahead and trust a little more today than you did yesterday.

- I trust you!
- I trust that you want to learn.
- I trust that you have amazing things to share, and I'm going to shape opportunities so that you can share them.

- I trust that you can learn from each other.
- I trust that our collective differences make us all a bit smarter.
- I trust that if you trust yourself, the best in you will come out.

Students Trusting Themselves

As the last bullet item in the preceding list suggests, your students don't only need to trust you and to know that you trust them; they also need to trust themselves. This is where building confidence comes in. Listen to the words of 6th grader Emily reflecting on her rising level of confidence that came from the validation she received after sharing her work with her classroom peers: "I felt comfortable and safe, because it was your ideas, so you're showing yourself. You should be proud of you and your ideas." Emily was learning to trust herself because her ideas had met with success. In a comfortable and safe environment, she was able to share her ideas and show herself. The same is true for another student who was in the process of learning to trust himself when he wrote, "I learned that I'm not as bad a reader as I thought I would be."

Trust also comes from genuine caring. The 8th grade team at Manheim Central Middle School meets daily for a team planning time. They share ideas, victories, and concerns over students. According to Matt Baker, "Our team does a good job of identifying students' problems early. If we see that there is a kid who needs help, we'll step in. For example, Mrs. Richards is always inviting kids to eat lunch with her. The kids know we talk about them and that we care. They are really comfortable because they know that we're here for them." When students know that you care about them, they're more likely to trust you.

Walking Around and Following Through

Trusting students doesn't mean that you relinquish accountability. Remember, the definition of a Total Participation Technique emphasizes that you gain *evidence* of active participation and cognitive engagement from each student at the same time. We trust that within carefully structured TPT activities students will shine, but the structured TPT has to be implemented. One of the easiest ways to make sure your TPTs fall flat is by not following through on your expectations for what students are supposed to be doing. If you ask students to complete a task, follow through by walking around, engaging students in quick content-based conversations, and responding to key words.

This not only allows you to get a feel for where students are in their learning progression, but it also keeps students accountable for completing their task. Students will quickly figure out whether or not their teachers are going to follow through on what they've asked their students to do. Many students know that when certain teachers ask them to do something, they don't really have to do it. No one is going to walk up to them, to remind them to participate. No one is even going to notice that they're not participating.

In the past few years, we have observed many lessons where a simple Thumb Up/Down Vote wasn't effective for the sole reason that only a few students voted. And the teacher, satisfied that the whole class had been given an opportunity to participate, simply moved on to the next topic. One Three 3's in a Row activity (see Figure 6.1) we observed resulted in a game of "pass the paper." Whereas the original intent of the activity is that students listen to each other and sum up their collective thinking, instead students simply passed the paper to the next person down the row and each student repeatedly wrote one of the nine responses of his or her choosing in the peer's box. There was minimal movement, no interaction between students, and minimal evidence of learning. For this activity, the lack of follow-through resulted in the opposite of what the teacher had intended.

How do you follow through? You don't have to penalize students or threaten consequences to get students to participate. Usually all you have to do is simply walk around, ask questions, and redirect students' attention ("Johnny, what are your thoughts on that?"). When students start realizing that you're going to keep them accountable, they'll start participating. It may take a little detoxification of old nonparticipatory habits, but with consistency it will happen. We've seen this at all grade levels and in all types of schools, whether urban, suburban, or rural. According to 5th grade teacher Mike Pyle, "When I have students who aren't used to working in groups, . . . it takes a while before they come to my class and know that they have to participate a lot. And they learn that they will be responsible to their team. It takes about a month before it comes naturally." It's important to know that your first attempts at interaction may seem forced, especially if students are not accustomed to interacting and working collaboratively. Courtney Cislo finds this to be true in her class. "In the beginning of the year, the same five kids have their hands up, but that changes as you use TPTs."

With time and the consistent use of Total Participation Techniques, classrooms can become a place where students not only enjoy the interaction, but expect it. Follow-through, however, is a necessary prerequisite. So if you expect students to participate, circulate and make comments regarding their interactions and input. Our jobs as teachers include not only planning for great teaching opportunities, but also ensuring that these opportunities result in student learning. As teachers, it is our job to ensure that our students actively participate and are cognitively engaged when they are within the boundaries of our classrooms. So when you implement a TPT, be sure to follow through on your expectations for all students.

Moving Away from Right/Wrong

In most scenarios that require students to display higher-order thinking, teachers will no longer be looking for the "right" answer. Instead, multiple possibilities often exist. Even when you ask a question with a set number of options, you are still looking for students to provide a rationale for why they chose their answer. Using evaluation, for example, your question might be "Which of these three habitats is most conducive to the life of this animal?" For the question to be considered an evaluation-type question, students have to justify their response based on learned content. The "how do you know?" has to be answered. In most cases, teachers will find that multiple responses or rationales will work. Once all students have had an opportunity to process the prompt individually and then in pairs or small groups, they will more likely be ready to share with the whole class. As you provide time for students to develop and discuss multiple responses and rationales, the dynamics of the classroom change. Students become invested in their different points of view and begin taking ownership over their own learning. They're no longer parroting back what you told them. Instead, students are thinking for themselves, connecting content to their implications, personal experiences, or other content learned.

When a teacher is looking for the "right" answer and a student says something that does not fit into what the teacher wanted the child to say, it is easy for the teacher to overlook the possibility that the child might have a sensible underlying rationale for the response. It is also easy to create a classroom environment where students no longer want to volunteer their responses because they fear that they have the wrong answer. Often in Potter's lessons, responses that might at first glance have seemed wrong added tremendous insight into the topic being discussed. According to Potter, "'Tell me more' is hands-down just about the best thing you can say." Those three simple words support a classroom environment of trust, placing the teacher in the role of a listener rather than an arbiter of truth. "Tell me more" allows students time to explain themselves. "Tell me more" can also help students, particularly in a math classroom, understand where they went wrong. It allows them to follow their own reasoning through to its logical or illogical conclusion, rather than being told by a peer or by a teacher. It allows them to scaffold backward, to where an error may have occurred in their line of reasoning. With "tell me more," students synthesize what they know and often answer their own questions. For incomplete thoughts, think about responding with an "I see where you're going with that." Give the student a few minutes to refine and polish the thought and bring it back to the class. Potter believes "you can reshape a student's thinking without shooting someone down. The first thing you do when you shoot somebody down is that they shut down." When students shut down, higher-order thinking suffers. According to Babcock, "As soon as you tell a kid that he's wrong, they stop thinking. When we brought our kids together, one of the things that surprised us was that the kids that were identified as Title I [struggling readers, in this case], they were so excited just to think. They felt smart; being in the classroom and giving them a voice just made them want to be there."

Reflection Questions

- What are your thoughts on the importance of student interaction?
- What have you noticed regarding students who do and do not experience success in your classroom?
- What are the dynamics of peer rejection and peer acceptance in your classroom? What role can you play in promoting peer acceptance?
- How is trust evident in your classroom? What can you do this week to increase the trust and student confidence in your classroom?
- How can trust and accountability coexist within a classroom?
- What pitfall do you see as the most important for teachers to avoid?
- If you had to add to this chapter one more essential ingredient for creating a TPT-conducive classroom, what would you add? Why?

Afterword

In this book, we've presented various activities that might be used to provide you with evidence of active participation and cognitive engagement. We'd like to leave you with a few thoughts, including how to avoid common pitfalls.

The Importance of Being Choosy

Not every Total Participation Technique we've presented is a good tool to use for every academic goal you have. Be selective. Choose the ones that are right for the particular learning goal you are shooting for. Some activities that could be characterized as TPTs aren't included in this book but may be perfect for spending time in Quadrant 4. Keep scouting for these in professional literature and add them to your toolkit. Follow-through isn't just for children; it's for all of us. Have high expectations for yourself, for planning with a purpose, for growing in your own understandings of the bigger implications of your content and how you help students understand these bigger implications. According to Keely Potter, "I could see the teachers falling into the same thing over and over again, like using a Pair-Share, and think they're doing Total Participation. To me the techniques are a way to get the content across, not the activity itself. The TPT is the portal, or the pathway, not the end in itself."

How to Avoid Common Pitfalls

When it comes to TPTs, it's easy to focus on the novelty of the techniques and the potential for spicing up otherwise dull lessons, but, believe it or not, the most important thing about Total Participation Techniques is *not* the techniques. TPTs are fun, but the goal is that students provide teachers with *evidence* that they are *cognitively engaged* with the content. This goal needs to be front and center, so that teachers can effectively use TPTs toward that end. The novelty and the fun ought to be viewed as by-products of students' cognitive engagement; they are not the main point. When educators focus on isolated techniques and fail to notice the big picture of their content, their efforts are short-lived and likely to be ineffective. To make a long-lasting impact on the cognitive engagement in your planning, be sure to avoid these common pitfalls that can sabotage your efforts toward deep and meaningful learning for all of your students.

Pitfall #1

Dismissal: "We're already doing that."

In our travels, we've come across educators who are quick to dismiss TPTs as something they don't need, because "we're already doing that." Recognizing the most commonly used TPT, the Think-Pair-Share, often leads educators to believe that there is little to be learned from understanding TPTs as a whole. The problem is that during consultant visits and walk-throughs, we often see very little by way of student engagement in the content presentations, and Think-Pair-Shares become old very quickly. (We need to add a disclaimer: We're guilty of this, too. It's easy to get caught up in teaching, because we understand or enjoy talking about the content, and lose focus of the students' lack of engagement.) Although it is very possible that educators are "already doing that," the best way of knowing whether or not this is true is to conduct a quadrant analysis. These can be done through video analysis or through peer collaboration and coaching. (See our website for helpful resources.) A quadrant analysis will help provide a more objective view of where students were engaged in the things that mattered, and where concepts could have been more deeply processed through the uses of TPTs.

Pitfall #2

Weak Prompts: The question wasn't worth the time invested.

Remember that the whole point of the Ripple (described in Chapter 2) is that students have time to process a question that requires higher-order thinking. If questions are weak or factual, you really don't need to ripple them. You may just want to have students quickly share the response with the person sitting next to them. TPTs are meant to help students learn deeply and become meaningfully engaged in learning the content, but not every question or concept is worth investing the extra time required to ripple questions. Reserve your rippled TPT structures for responses that will require higher-order thinking.

Pitfall #3

Prioritizing the Method: The technique becomes the lesson.

Many Total Participation Techniques are fun and interactive, which might lead some teachers to select the TPT first and then shape a lesson around it. Unfortunately, doing so can result in students learning the various steps involved in conducting the TPT, but they might learn very little about the content. Although the students might interact and enjoy themselves, very little of the learning target might be met. Instead, if your goal is to make the content meaningful, your content goals should be selected first. Once you've decided what specific content you'd like to teach, then select a TPT that is best suited toward meeting that content goal at deep levels of understanding. Be sure to take some time to create meaningful questions or prompts that will allow your students to explore the content at a deeper level.

Pitfall #4

Monotony: We get stuck in a rut.

You may find your comfort zone with a handful of techniques that are presented in this book. In one way, that's a good thing; you ought to choose techniques that fit your teaching style and personality. Just be careful not to get stuck in a rut. Students get tired of doing the same activities day in and day out. Instead, revisit the techniques presented in this book, modify them, make them your own, and add to them. Use sticky notes for techniques that sound interesting and that you'd like to revisit but aren't yet sure how to fit into your lesson plans. As you're planning your units, have this book in hand. What techniques will add to students' understanding of the content? Even though we wrote this book, we fall into the trap of getting stuck in a rut, too. However, our teaching dramatically improves when we go back with fresh eyes to revisit the techniques, and when we force ourselves to get outside our comfort zones and add new TPTs to our teaching repertoire. We encourage you to do the same.

The Power of TPTs

We really believe in the power of Total Participation Techniques. We even believe that if all teachers were to actively focus on the two components of TPTs—active participation by all and higher-order thinking (see Figure 2.1)—our schools could be dynamic and exciting places where student learning takes front and center stage. We believe that through the consistent use of TPTs, we could reduce the dropout and failure rate among students. And we would support students in exploring deeper understandings that can build the academic confidence that will help them to succeed in school and life. We have seen the difference that TPTs can make in student engagement and learning, and the improved on-task behavior that results from the implementation of TPTs.

We strongly believe that TPTs can make us all better teachers. The most exciting outcome that we have seen through the implementation of TPTs is that students shine. According to Meghan Babcock, "These TPTs have really tightened up what Keely and I do together, and the kids have risen to the expectations that we've set for them." When you give students the opportunity to demonstrate higher-order thinking and to learn through individual processing followed by interaction, they will surprise you. It is our hope that this text will inspire and support you in building the cognitively engaging classrooms that children crave.

Appendix A: Higher-Order Thinking and Depth of Knowledge

The TPT Cognitive Engagement Model (described in Chapter 2) focuses on evidence of participation by all students with tasks that require higher-order thinking. We'd like to address a common question that has been brought up by teachers with whom we work: *"How do TPTs work if our school is emphasizing the use of Webb's Depth of Knowledge as opposed to Bloom's taxonomy and higher-order thinking?"* At times the question is phrased in a way that leads us to believe that there is a great deal of confusion between Bloom's taxonomy and Webb's Depth of Knowledge (DOK). One of the most common misunderstandings is the underlying assumption that Webb's DOK and Bloom's taxonomy are interchangeable and essentially do the same things. In this Appendix, we'd like to address this by first introducing Bloom's original and revised taxonomies, and then discussing Webb's DOK. We'll also explain how the two differ.

One of the biggest challenges associated with understanding and assessing cognition is to select a model that can account for the complexities involved in learning, while also being simple enough to use. Educators don't always agree on what constitutes a useful model or framework, and schools will often emphasize the use of a model in order to support the creation of a common language. In the following sections, we present two models that have attempted to somewhat quantify the complex qualities of learning.

Bloom's Original Taxonomy

More than 50 years ago, Benjamin Bloom and his colleagues (1956) developed a handbook that introduced a cognitive taxonomy (or classification system) of educational objectives. Bloom's original taxonomy consists of six levels, divided into *lower-order thinking* and *higher-order thinking*. The lower-order thinking classifications are divided up into Knowledge, Comprehension, and Application. The higher-order thinking classifications consist of Analysis, Synthesis, and Evaluation. This taxonomy is still valuable and in use in many schools today. While Bloom and his associates acknowledged the taxonomy's simplicity, recent attempts to make up for its perceived limitations have led to notable revisions (Anderson et al., 2014; Marzano & Kendall, 2007).

Bloom's Revised Taxonomy

One of the teams that took on a revision of the handbook included Lorin Anderson, a former student of Bloom, and David Krathwohl, who served as one of the original authors for the 1956 taxonomy. In the revised handbook, greater emphasis was placed on the four types of knowledge: factual, conceptual, procedural, and metacognitive (*metacognitive knowledge* was not present in the original handbook). The lens of the revision was changed from one that focused on assessment to one that focused on the alignment of curricular planning, instruction, and assessment. The focus also changed from that of higher education to a focus on K–12 teachers. Greater emphasis was also placed on the overlap of cognitive complexities.

With regard to the six main categories of the taxonomy, the nouns that had been present in the original 1956 taxonomy were changed to verbs in order to reflect how they are used in teaching objectives. The six major categories are described within 19 subcategories, which take on added significance in the revised taxonomy. Additionally, the scope of the category Comprehension/Understand was expanded, and includes some subcategories with increased complexity (Krathwohl, 2002). Finally, the categories of Synthesis/Create and Evaluation/Evaluate were reversed, assigning greater complexity to Synthesis/Create. Figure A.1 outlines some of the differences in the six major categories of the taxonomy.

Webb's Depth of Knowledge

One of the more well-known curricular/cognitive depth models that has become widespread in recent years is Norman Webb's Depth of Knowledge (1997, 2002, 2007). It is not so much a *cognitive* depth model as it is a *curricular* depth model, because it does not focus on describing cognitive

Figure A.1

Bloom's Original and Revised Taxonomies

The Original Taxonomy (Bloom et al., 1956) The various dimensions of knowledge, except for the metacognitive, were addressed but not emphasized.	The Revised Taxonomy (Anderson et al., 2014) Four *Knowledge Dimensions* are addressed and emphasized. They are Factual Knowledge, Conceptual Knowledge, Procedural Knowledge, and Metacognitive Knowledge.
Knowledge refers to "remembering, either by recognition or recall" (Bloom et al., 1956, p. 62). It usually takes only a few words to answer a question aimed at knowledge, and the answer does not require any connection making on the part of the learners. They're simply giving you back what you taught them. For example, you might ask, "How many sides does a hexagon have?"	**Remember** is described by the two subcategories: *Recognizing* and *Recalling*. *Recognizing* refers to locating knowledge in long-term memory, while *Recalling* refers to retrieving relevant knowledge in long-term memory. For example, if students are matching given dates with given events, they are being asked to recognize; if they are being asked to tell the dates (not given) for given events, they are being asked to recall.
Comprehension "represents the lowest level of understanding. It refers to a type of understanding or apprehension such that the individual knows what is being communicated and can make use of the material or idea being communicated without necessarily relating it to other material or seeing its fullest implications" (Bloom et al., 1956, p. 204). In the original taxonomy, Bloom and others explain "It differs from application, however, in that the thinking is based on what is given rather than on some abstraction brought from the other experiences to the situation, such as a general principle or rule of procedure" (p. 90). In the revised taxonomy, the scope is broadened.	**Understand** is described by these seven subcategories: *Interpreting, Exemplifying, Classifying, Summarizing, Inferring, Comparing,* and *Explaining*. The subcategories spell out more detailed ways that students construct meaning. More comfort with overlap, rather than hierarchy, is noted in this category. In the revision, "some cognitive processes associated with *Understand* (e. g. *Explaining*) are more cognitively complex than at least one of the cognitive processes associated with *Apply*" (Krathwohl, 2002, p. 215). Krathwohl notes that the hierarchy becomes more visible as one looks at the "center point" of each of the six major categories.
Application refers to "the use of abstractions in particular and concrete situations" (Bloom et al., 1956, p. 205). With goals aimed at the application level, students are simply using or applying what you taught them. *Application* still does not require them to develop abstractions of their own. For example, if you're teaching the area of a rectangle, *Application* might involve asking students to simply plug in numbers using an abstract formula that you gave them. The learning becomes *Synthesis*, a higher-order thinking classification, when they develop their own formulas (abstractions) that are new to them (even if these formulas aren't new to you).	**Apply** is described by these two subcategories: *Executing* and *Implementing*. *Executing* refers to applying a procedure to a familiar task, such as dividing a whole two-digit number by another whole two-digit number. *Implementing* refers to applying a procedure to an unfamiliar task, such as using "Newton's Second Law in situations in which it is appropriate" (Anderson et al., 2014, p. 67). This category is often mistaken for *Create*, however as with the original 1956 category, when it comes to *Apply*, students are using a learned procedure in a familiar or unfamiliar task, but they are not creating new procedures.

continued

Figure A.1 (*continued*)
Bloom's Original and Revised Taxonomies

Analysis refers to "the breakdown of a communication into its constituent elements or parts such that the relative hierarchy of ideas is made clear or the relations between the ideas expressed are made explicit" (Bloom et al., 1956, p. 205). To analyze, students have to understand the nuances within a concept. They have to be able to make connections between ideas and look at how these ideas affect each other.	**Analyze** is described by these three categories: *Differentiating*, *Organizing*, and *Attributing*. *Differentiating* refers to "distinguishing relevant from irrelevant parts … of presented materials" (Anderson et al., 2014, p. 69). *Organizing* refers to "determining how elements fit or function within a structure" (p. 69). *Attributing* refers to "determining a point of view, bias, values, or intent underlying presented material" (p. 69).
Synthesis refers to "the putting together of elements and parts so as to form a whole. This involves the process of working with pieces, parts, elements, etc., and arranging and combining them in such a way as to constitute a pattern or structure not clearly there before" (Bloom et al., 1956, p. 206). The key with *Synthesis* is that the abstraction, pattern, or new structure comes from the student, not the teacher (see the earlier *Application* example for mathematics).	**Evaluate** is described by the two subcategories, *Checking* and *Critiquing*. *Checking* involves determining whether inconsistencies, fallacies, or internal consistencies exist, while *Critiquing* involves determining inconsistencies based on external criteria. For both *Checking* and *Critiquing*, students are being asked to do so within the boundaries of certain criteria and standards.
Evaluation refers to "quantitative and qualitative judgments about the extent to which material and methods satisfy criteria" (Bloom et al., 1956, p. 207). It does not simply refer to students giving their opinion. For the task to qualify as *Evaluation*, the judgment has to make use of and be based on learned material.	**Create** is described by the three subcategories, *Generating*, *Planning*, and *Producing*. *Generating* involves creating new hypotheses based on criteria. *Planning* involves creating a procedure for accomplishing a task. *Producing* involves inventing a product. As with the original taxonomy, within the *Create* category, students are being asked to use what they've learned to develop something new, not copying existing models.

processes—a task undertaken by Bloom and others, as well as by educational psychologists—rather, it focuses on describing the types of curricular tasks in which we involve our students. Webb's research often examines Depth of Knowledge consistency, which looks at the alignment between standards and assessments. According to Webb, "DOK consistency between standards and assessment indicates alignment if what is elicited from students on the assessment is as demanding cognitively as what students are expected to know and do as stated in the standards" (2007, p. 11).

In order to measure the various levels of depth in a standard and its corresponding assessment, Webb developed four descriptions that are categorized by levels. Unlike Bloom's levels, they are nonhierarchical, because a higher level does not require mastery of a lower level. The intent of Webb's DOK is also different from that of Bloom's taxonomy. Instead of describing a skill, Webb analyzes tasks and the cognitive complexity inherent in the context of these tasks. These tasks may involve several of the skills described by Bloom and others.

The four levels of Webb's DOK are as follows:

DOK Level 1 (Recall)
Recall of a fact, information or procedure

DOK Level 2 (Application of Skills and Concepts)
Use of information, conceptual knowledge, procedures, two or more steps, etc.

DOK Level 3 (Strategic Thinking)
Requires reasoning, developing a plan or sequences of steps; has some complexity; more than one possible answer; generally takes less than 10 minutes to do

DOK Level 4 (Extended Thinking)
Requires an investigation; time to think and process multiple conditions of the problem or task; and more than 10 minutes to do non-routine manipulations (Webb, 1999, p. 3)

Typically, Level 4 projects are assigned over an extended period of time. Involving students in tasks that are characterized by Level 4 is ideal, because it "requires complex reasoning, planning, developing, and thinking most likely over an extended period of time" (Webb, 2007, p. 12). Webb further explains that the extended period of time is not an indicator of depth when the extended period of time is spent doing repetitive tasks that do not require complex reasoning. He describes one such task and what it might take for that same task to be identified as a Level 4 task. "If a student has to take the water temperature from a river each day for a month and then construct a graph, this would be classified at Level 2. However, if the student is to conduct a river study that requires taking into consideration a number of variables, this would be at Level 4. At Level 4, the demands of the task should be high and the work should be very complex" (p. 13). Note how a high-DOK-level task may involve the use of skills that could be characterized by several or all six of the categories in Bloom's taxonomy.

Bloom versus Webb

Understanding the distinction between Webb's Depth of Knowledge and Bloom's taxonomy can lead to much confusion. Below are some concepts to keep in mind when trying to understand Webb's DOK as it relates to Bloom's taxonomy.

- Webb's DOK is not a rewrite of Bloom's taxonomy. It's not an improved reorganizing or relabeling of Bloom's taxonomy.
- The DOK levels are not sequential or placed in a hierarchy, as are the levels in Bloom's taxonomy. Though the higher levels often provide more depth, a Level 3 task may actually be more complex than a Level 4 task (Webb, 2014). This is possibly the most misunderstood concept as it relates to Webb's DOK. Rather than think of DOK as a line-up of least complex to more complex tasks, it may help to consider Webb's DOK as a compilation of categories and curricular possibilities. They are not linear in nature.
- Where DOK is concerned, Webb addresses the impracticality of expecting to assign Level 4 tasks on a daily basis (Webb, 2014). Level 4 tasks are time intensive and are typically projects that stretch over several days. In contrast, one can expect to use all six categories of Bloom's taxonomy on a daily basis.
- The purpose of DOK is different than that of Bloom's taxonomy. Instead of summarizing or defining levels of cognitive depth in questions, it takes on more complexity by examining the context in which the students are practicing the skills and the level of understanding that is necessary in order to complete curricular tasks that often involve several skills, and it may involve several days.
- DOK attempts to assess how well curriculum and standards are aligned to assessment tasks. Although its uses and applications stretched beyond assessment, Bloom's original taxonomy (1956) attempted to assess the cognitive depth in assessment items. The revised taxonomy and its handbook (Anderson et al., 2014) explicitly attempt to support planning, instruction, and assessment in K–12 classrooms.
- DOK and Bloom's taxonomy are not mutually exclusive. Because they serve different purposes, they can both be used at the same time, together.

We are finding that Webb's DOK is most useful for helping teachers analyze the complexity of the depth of content learning necessary to successfully complete curricular tasks, and to assess whether or not the curricular tasks are aligned to the expectations inherent in their standards. Bloom's taxonomy is most useful for planning and developing prompts that are aimed at eliciting deeper thinking on the part of students. Although they both are used by teachers to improve the cognitive depth of their teaching, Webb's DOK is more global in nature, analyzing cognitive depth within the larger contexts of categories of curricular tasks (think of the types of assignments that might be listed in a high school or college syllabus), while Bloom's taxonomy is more discrete, focusing on the cognitive depth that is intended mostly by the prompts and questions within the tasks (think of those types of tasks that are featured within your lesson plan for today).

Numerous additional cognitive and curricular depth models exist with the goal of articulating what deep student learning should look like. Though we've only discussed two here, most approaches provide a different angle that can shed light on our understanding of complex cognitive process.

Useful Resources for Increasing Depth in Your Classroom

In her book *How to Assess Higher-Order Thinking Skills in Your Classroom*, Susan Brookhart provides an overview of various cognitive models and ways to assess for higher-order thinking. She uses the following categories to illustrate properties of what would be considered higher-order thinking:

- Analysis, evaluation, and creation (the top end of Bloom's taxonomy)
- Logical reasoning
- Judgment and critical thinking
- Problem solving
- Creativity and creative thinking (Brookhart, 2010, p. 14)

Her book provides helpful insights for understanding what higher-order thinking looks like and how to ensure that it is happening in your classroom.

In his book *Now That's a Good Question!*, Erik Francis provides concrete examples that combine both higher-order thinking and Webb's Depth of Knowledge to guide educators through understanding how they might "promote cognitive rigor by providing students with the opportunity to demonstrate and communicate their knowledge and thinking at the highest level of Bloom's taxonomy (analyze, evaluate, create) and deepest levels of Webb's model (strategic and extended thinking)" (2016, p. 162). His book offers helpful tools that can assist educators in better understanding cognitive rigor and how to create learning opportunities through the power of excellent prompts.

How Do TPTs Fit with Bloom and Webb?

As noted earlier, there are several useful taxonomies and models aimed at understanding human cognition and the quality of our curriculum that we haven't touched on here. These models can help raise questions regarding quality learning opportunities, and they can provide assistance in helping us deepen the cognitive investment on the part of our students.

The TPT Cognitive Engagement Model (described in Chapter 2) is meant to assist teachers in providing cognitively engaging learning opportunities that ensure total participation and deeper learning for every student within every lesson. Although the techniques described in this book will ensure active participation on the part of all students, the quality of the learning is heavily dependent on the power of your questions and prompts. This is why we follow the procedural explanations of each of the techniques with a description of "How to Ensure Higher-Order Thinking."

With regard to Bloom's taxonomy, we are shooting for questions and prompts that require students to analyze, evaluate, and create or synthesize using the content that has been learned during that lesson or unit. If your school emphasizes the use of DOK, then Quadrant 4 of the TPT Cognitive Engagement Model helps you select tasks that focus on higher-order thinking within curricular tasks that involve mostly Strategic Thinking (Level 3) and, at times, Extended Thinking (Level 4).

This book provides strategies that would be used during the course of a lesson. Because time is often an issue, many of the tools are going to support you in helping your students function in curricular tasks that are described by Strategic Thinking (Level 3). In Level 3, students are required to reason, analyze, create, and synthesize the content that they are learning within an activity that can be completed in a relatively brief period of time. Depending on the activity, some of your TPTs might also be characterized by Extended Thinking (Level 4). Again, it's not practical to expect to assign Level 4 tasks on a daily basis (Webb, 2014). To make learning truly meaningful, you will want to select Level 4 tasks that are cognitively complex and that may stretch over several days. However, where TPTs are concerned, students should be operating in Quadrant 4 at least once every lesson.

As new cognitive models continue to be introduced over the coming decades, they can provide further insight into how to ensure that our students are engaged in learning that is deep, meaningful, and lasting. The key thing to remember is that those deeper learning opportunities need to be made available to *every* student, not just a few. Regardless of how you approach analyzing the quality of your curriculum, Total Participation Techniques can help you achieve the lofty goal of ensuring that all students are engaged in deeper learning before they exit your classroom.

Appendix B: Posters and Tools

This appendix contains tools and mini-posters that are on-the-spot reminders about adding TPTs when you are teaching and planning lessons. Some of the posters are conceptual in nature. They remind you to ripple or that the question stem, "Who can tell me . . . ?" can be improved upon by adding individual accountability.

The lists are aimed at reminding you of TPTs that take minimal preparation. Post them in places that will help you to remember to use them and refer to this book as a reminder about how each technique works.

1. The TPT Quadrants
2. The Ripple
3. Think Before You Ask, "Who can tell me . . . ?"
4. Quick TPTs for Early Childhood Classrooms
5. No-Prep and Low-Prep TPTs
6. Bounce Cards
7. Appointment Agendas
8. Hold-Up Cards
9. The Trust Poem

Readers may duplicate items in Appendix B for noncommercial use within their school. Downloadable versions of some forms are available at this URL: www.ascd.org/ASCD/pdf/books/himmele2017.pdf

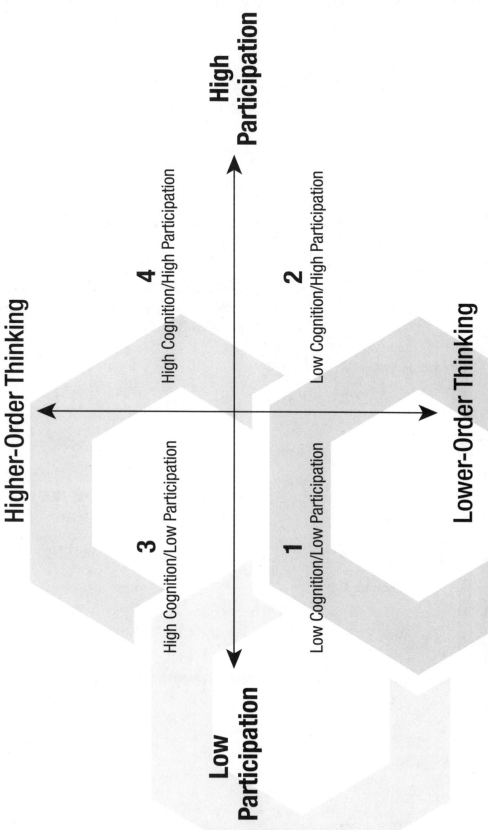

The TPT Quadrants

Higher-Order Thinking

High Participation

4 High Cognition/High Participation

2 Low Cognition/High Participation

3 High Cognition/Low Participation

1 Low Cognition/Low Participation

Low Participation

Lower-Order Thinking

THE RIPPLE

The Ripple is a cornerstone to understanding how to create and implement Total Participation Techniques.

Volunteers or selected students share with the whole class. ③

Students share responses in pairs or small groups. ②

All students respond individually to a higher-order prompt. ①

The Ripple **IS** a way of posing questions to maximize actual learning time.	The Ripple **IS NOT** a traditional Q & A session.
The Ripple **IS** a way to engage each and every student.	The Ripple **IS NOT** calling on an individual student for the answer.
The Ripple **IS** all students responding to a prompt using Quick-Writes or other TPT structures.	The Ripple **IS NOT** simply group work.
The Ripple **IS** beneficial for all students, especially English language learners, socially tentative students, and students with special needs.	The Ripple **IS NOT** intimidating and does not put students "on the spot."

Source: © 2017 ASCD. From *Total Participation Techniques: Making Every Student an Active Learner,* 2nd edition, by Pérsida and William Himmele. Readers may duplicate blackline masters and posters for noncommercial use within their school.

Think, before you ask, "Who can tell me…?"

Who can tell me…?

Remember to Ripple!

Calling on someone should be the **last** thing that you do.

Quick TPTs for Early Childhood Classrooms

- ## Mouth It
- ## Air-Write It
- ## Whisper It to a Neighbor
- ## Write It on the Carpet
- ## Point to It
- ## Show Me Using Your Fingers

No-Prep and Low-Prep TPTs

- **Chalkboard Splash**
- **IQ Cards**
- **One-Word Summary**
- **Pause, Star, Rank**
- **Confer, Compare, Clarify**
- **Quick-Writes**
- **Quick-Draws**
- **Picture Notes**
- **Biggest *Aha!***
- **Biggest *Aha* Bar Graph**

Bounce Card

Bounce

Take what your classmate(s) said and bounce an idea off of it. For example, start your sentence with

"That reminds me of . . . "
"I agree, because . . . "
"True, another example is when . . . "
"That's a great point . . . "

Sum It Up

Rephrase what was just said in a shorter version. For example, you can start your sentences with

"I hear you saying that . . . "
"So, if I understand you correctly . . . "
"I like how you said . . . "

Ask a Question

Understand what your classmates mean by asking questions. For example, you can start your questions with

"Can you tell me more about that?"
"I see your point, but what about . . . ?"
"Have you thought about . . . ?"

Bounce Card

Bounce

Take what your classmate(s) said and bounce an idea off of it. For example, start your sentence with

"That reminds me of . . . "
"I agree, because . . . "
"True, another example is when . . . "
"That's a great point . . . "

Sum It Up

Rephrase what was just said in a shorter version. For example, you can start your sentences with

"I hear you saying that . . . "
"So, if I understand you correctly . . . "
"I like how you said . . . "

Ask a Question

Understand what your classmates mean by asking questions. For example, you can start your questions with

"Can you tell me more about that?"
"I see your point, but what about . . . ?"
"Have you thought about . . . ?"

Appointments for _____	
Time	**You have an appointment with**
8:00 am	
9:00 am	
10:00 am	
11:00 am	
12:00 pm	
1:00 pm	
2:00 pm	
3:00 pm	
4:00 pm	
5:00 pm	
6:00 pm	
7:00 pm	
8:00 pm	

Appointments for _____	
Time	**You have an appointment with**
8:00 am	
9:00 am	
10:00 am	
11:00 am	
12:00 pm	
1:00 pm	
2:00 pm	
3:00 pm	
4:00 pm	
5:00 pm	
6:00 pm	
7:00 pm	
8:00 pm	

NOT TRUE

UNABLE TO DETERMINE
based on information learned

TRUE

TRUE
WITH MODIFICATIONS

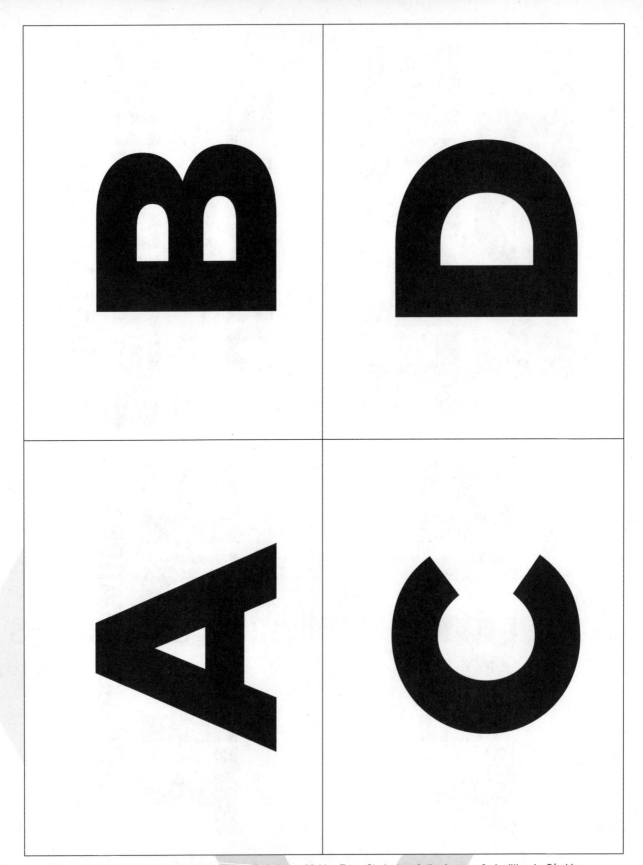

The Trust Poem

I trust you!

I trust that you want to learn.

I trust that you have
amazing things to share,

and I'm going to shape
opportunities so that you
can share them.

I trust that you can learn
from each other.

I trust that our collective differences
make us all a bit smarter.

I trust that if you trust yourself,
the best in you will come out.

Source: © 2017 ASCD. From *Total Participation Techniques: Making Every Student an Active Learner,* 2nd edition, by Pérsida and William Himmele. Readers may duplicate blackline masters and posters for noncommercial use within their school.

References

America's Promise Alliance. (2014). *Don't call them dropouts: Understanding the experiences of young people who leave high school before graduation.* Medford, MA: Center for Promise, Tufts University.

Anderson, L. W., et al. (2014). *A taxonomy for learning, teaching, and assessing: A revision of Bloom's taxonomy of educational objectives* (Pearson New International Edition). Essex, UK: Pearson Education.

ASCD. (2010). *Legislative agenda.* Retrieved June 25, 2010, from http://www.ascd.org/public-policy/Legislative-Agenda/Legislative-Agenda.aspx

Balfanz, R., Bridgeland, J., Moore, L., & Hornig Fox, J. (2010). *Building a grad nation: Progress and challenge in ending the high school dropout epidemic.* A report by Civic Enterprises, Everyone Graduates Center at Johns Hopkins University, and America's Promise Alliance.

Ball, M., & Cerullo, J. (2004). *It takes courage: Promoting character and healthy life choices.* Harrisonburg, VA: Kerus Global Publishing.

Bartiromo, M. (2010). *The 10 laws of enduring success.* New York: Crown Business.

Black, D. W. (2016). Taking teacher quality seriously. *William & Mary Law Review, 57*(5), 1597–1669.

Black, P., & Wiliam, D. (1998, March). Assessment and classroom learning. *Assessment in Education: Principles, Policy & Practice, 5*(1), 7–74.

Bloom, B. S., Englehart, M. D., Furst, E. J., Hill, W. H., & Krathwohl, R. R. (Eds.). (1956). *Taxonomy of educational objectives: The classification of educational goals. Handbook 1, Cognitive domain.* New York: McKay.

Bridgeland, J. M., DiIulio, J. J., Jr., & Morison, K. B. (2006). *The silent epidemic: Perspectives of high school dropouts.* Washington, DC: Civic Enterprises.

Brookhart, S. (2010). *How to assess higher-order thinking skills in your classroom.* Alexandria, VA: ASCD.

Bunce, D. M., Flens, E. A., & Neiles, K. Y. (2010). How long can students pay attention in class? A study of student attention decline using clickers. *Journal of Chemical Education, 87*(12), 1438–1443.

Certo, J. L., Cauley, K. M., Moxley, K. D., & Chafin, C. (2008, April/ May). An argument for authenticity: Adolescents' perspectives on standards-based reform. *The High School Journal, 91*(4), 26–39.

Chambers, T. V. (2009). The "receivement gap": School tracking policies and the fallacy of the "achievement gap." *Journal of Negro Education, 78*(4), 417–431.

Christle, C. A., & Schuster, J. W. (2003, September). The effects of using response cards on student participation, academic achievement, and on-task behavior during whole-class math instruction. *Journal of Behavioral Education, 12*(3), 147–165.

Clayton, M. C., & Woodard, C. (2007, September). The effect of response cards on participation and weekly quiz scores of university students enrolled in introductory psychology courses. *Journal of Behavioral Education, 16*(3), 250–258.

Corbitt, C., & Carpenter, M. (2006, March). The nervous system game. *Science and Children, 43*(6), 26–29.

Darling-Hammond, L. (2000). Teacher quality and student achievement: A review of state policy evidence. *Education Policy Analysis Archives, 8*(1).

de la Isla, A. (2015). *Total participation techniques to increase academic language in English language learners.* (Unpublished doctoral dissertation.) Dallas Baptist University: Dallas, TX.

DePaoli, J. L., Balfanz, R., & Bridgeland, J. (2016). *Building a grad nation: Progress and challenge in raising high school graduation rates.* A report by Civic Enterprises, Everyone Graduates Center at Johns Hopkins University, and America's Promise Alliance.

DiCamillo, K. (2001) *The tiger rising.* New York: Scholastic.

Dykman, B. M., & Reis, H. T. (1979). Personality correlates of classroom seating position. *Journal of Educational Psychology, 71*(3), 346–354.

Ferguson, B. (August, 2016). Total Participation Techniques with two sample activities. [Blog post.] Available: http://algebrasfriend.blogspot.com/2016/08/mtbosblaugust-total-participation.html

Francis, E. (2016). *Now that's a good question! How to promote cognitive rigor through classroom questioning.* Alexandria, VA: ASCD.

Freire, P. (2000). *Pedagogy of the oppressed* (30th anniversary edition). New York: Continuum International Publishing Group Inc. (Original work published 1970.)

Funke, C. (2001). *The thief lord.* New York: Scholastic.

Gallup, Inc. (2015). *Gallup student poll: Engaged today, ready for tomorrow. Fall 2015 scorecard.* Gallup, Inc.

Harlow, C. W. (2003). *Education and correctional populations: Bureau of Justice Statistics special report.* Washington, DC: U.S. Department of Justice. Retrieved July 1, 2010, from www.ojp.usdoj.gov/bjs/pub/pdf/ecp.pdf

Himmele, P., & Himmele, W. (2009). *The language-rich classroom: A research-based framework for teaching English language learners.* Alexandria, VA: ASCD.

Himmele, P., & Himmele, W. (2011). *Total participation techniques: Making every student an active learner* (1st ed.). Alexandria, VA: ASCD.

Himmele, P., Himmele, W., & Potter, K. (2014). *Total literacy techniques: Tools to help students analyze literature and informational texts.* Alexandria, VA: ASCD.

Jordan, H. R., Mendro, R. L., & Weerasinghe, D. (1997). *Teacher effects on longitudinal student achievement: A report on research in progress.* Paper presented at the CREATE Annual Meeting, Indianapolis, IN.

Kagan, S. (December 1989/January 1990). The structural approach to cooperative learning. *Educational Leadership, 47*(4), 12–15.

Klein, R. (2008, March). Engaging students around the globe. *Educational Leadership, 65*(5), 8–13.

Konrad, M., Joseph, L. M., & Eveleigh, E. (2009, August). A meta-analytic review of guided notes. *Education & Treatment of Children, 32*(3), 421–444.

Krathwohl, D. R. (2002). A revision of Bloom's taxonomy: An overview. *Theory in Practice, 41*(4). College of Education, Ohio State University.

Ladd, G. W., Herald-Brown, S. L., & Reiser, M. (2008, July/August). Does chronic classroom peer rejection predict the development of children's classroom participation during the grade school years? *Child Development, 79*(4), 1001–1015.

Lahtinen, V., Lonka, K., & Lindblom-Ylänne, S. (1997). Spontaneous study strategies and the quality of knowledge construction. *British Journal of Educational Psychology, 67*(1), 13–24.

Lambert, M. C., Cartledge, G., Heward, W. L., & Lo, Y. (2006). Effects of response cards on disruptive behavior and academic responding during math lessons by fourth-grade urban students. *Journal of Positive Behavior Interventions, 8*(2), 88–99.

Lee, P., Lan, W., Hamman, D., & Hendricks, B. (2008, May). The effects of teaching notetaking strategies on elementary students' science learning. *Instructional Science, 36*(3), 191–201.

Lehr, C. A., Johnson, D. R., Bremer, C. D., Cosio, A., & Thompson, M. (2004). *Essential tools: Increasing rates of school completion.* Minneapolis, MN: National Center on Secondary Education and Transition. Retrieved June 30, 2010, from http://www.ecs.org/html/Document.asp?chouseid=6649

Lehrer, J. (January 30, 2012). Groupthink: The brainstorming myth. *The New Yorker.* Available: http://www.newyorker.com/magazine/2012/01/30/groupthink

Luehmann, A., & MacBride, R. (2009). Classroom blogging in the service of student-centered pedagogy: Two high school teachers' use of blogs. *THEN Technology, Humanities, Education, & Narrative,* Issue 6.

Lyman, F. T. (1981). The responsive classroom discussion: The inclusion of all students. In A. Anderson (Ed.), *Mainstreaming Digest* (pp. 109–113). College Park, MD: University of Maryland Press.

Marshall, K. (2009, May). A how-to plan for widening the gap. *Phi Delta Kappan, 90*(9), 650–655.

Martin, N., & Halperin, S. (2006). *Whatever it takes: How twelve communities are reconnecting out-of-school youth.* Washington, DC: Civic Enterprises.

Marzano, R. J., & Kendall, J. S. (2007). *The new taxonomy of educational objectives* (2nd ed.). Thousand Oaks, CA: Corwin Press.

Meehan, M. L. (1999). *Evaluation of the Monongalia County Schools' Even Start program child vocabulary outcomes.* Charleston, WV: AEL.

Moretti, E. (2005, October). *Does education reduce participation in criminal activities?* Paper presented at the Symposium on the Social Costs of Inadequate Education, Teachers College, Columbia University, New York.

Munro, D. W., & Stephenson, J. (2009). The effects of response cards on student and teacher behavior during vocabulary instruction. *Journal of Applied Behavioral Analysis, 42*(4), 795–800.

Musti-Rao, S., Kroeger, S. D., & Schumacher-Dyke, K. (2008). Using guided notes and response cards at the postsecondary level. *Teacher Education & Special Education, 31*(3), 149–163.

Nichols, P. D., Meyers, J. L., & Burling, K. S. (2009, September). A framework for evaluating and planning assessments intended to improve student achievement. *Educational Measurement: Issues & Practice, 28*(3), 14–23.

Randolph, J. J. (2007). Meta-analysis of the research on response cards: Effects in test achievement, quiz achievement, participation, and off-task behavior. *Journal of Positive Behavior Interventions, 9*(2), 113–128.

Ream, R. K., & Rumberger, R. W. (2008, April). Student engagement, peer social capital, and school dropout among Mexican American and non-Latino white students. *Sociology of Education, 81,* 109–139.

Rennie Center for Education Research & Policy. (2012, November). *Forgotten youth: Re-engaging students through dropout recovery.* Cambridge, MA: Rennie Center for Education Research & Policy.

Reutzel, D. R., & Cooter, R. B., Jr. (2015). *Teaching children to read: The teacher makes the difference* (7th ed.). Upper Saddle River, NJ: Pearson.

Roberts, T. (2008). Home storybook reading in primary or second language with preschool children: Evidence of equal effectiveness for second language vocabulary acquisition. *Reading Research Quarterly, 43*(2), 103–130.

Rumberger, R. W. (2008, February). *Solving California's dropout crisis: California Dropout Research Project policy committee report.* Santa Barbara, CA: UC Linguistic Minority Research Institute and the Gevirtz Graduate School of Education at the University of California, Santa Barbara.

Sanders, W. L., & Horn, S. P. (1998). Research findings from the Tennessee Value-Added Assessment System (TVAAS) database: Implications for educational evaluation and research. *Journal of Personnel Evaluation in Education, 12*(3), 247–256.

Sanders, W. L., & Rivers, J. C. (1996). *Cumulative and residual effects of teachers on future student achievement: Research progress report.* Knoxville, TN: University of Tennessee Value-Added Research and Assessment Center.

Sénéchal, M., & LeFevre, J. A. (2002). Parental involvement in the development of children's reading skill: A five-year longitudinal study. *Child Development, 73*(2), 445–460.

Sharif, I., Ozuah, P. O., Dinkevich, E. I., & Mulvihill, M. (2003). Impact of a brief literacy intervention on urban preschoolers. *Early Childhood Education Journal, 30*(3), 177–180.

Sousa, D. A. (2006). *How the brain learns* (3rd ed.). Thousand Oaks, CA: Corwin Press.

Strauss, V. (2014, October 24). Teacher spends two days as a student and is shocked at what she learns. *Washington Post: Answer Sheet.*

Taba, H. (1967). *Teacher's handbook for elementary social studies.* Reading, MA: Addison-Wesley.

Tanner, J. (1990). Reluctant rebels: A case study of Edmonton high school dropouts. *Canadian Review of Sociology & Anthropology, 27*(1), 74–94.

Tucker, P. D., & Stronge, J. H. (2005). *Linking teacher evaluation and student learning.* Alexandria, VA: ASCD.

Voke, H. (2002, February). Motivating students to learn. *Infobrief* (No. 28). Retrieved July 11, 2010, from http://www.ascd.org/publications/newsletters/infobrief/feb02/num28/Motivating-Students-to-Learn.aspx

Webb, N. (1997). *Criteria for alignment of expectations and assessments in mathematics and science education.* Research Monograph No. 6. Council of Chief State School Officers and National Institute for Science Education. Madison, WI: University of Wisconsin, Wisconsin Center for Education Research.

Webb, N. (1999). *Alignment of science and mathematics standards and assessments in four states.* Research Monograph No. 18. Council of Chief State School Officers and National Institute for Science Education. Madison, WI: University of Wisconsin, Wisconsin Center for Education Research.

Webb, N. (2002). *Depth of knowledge levels for four content areas* (Unpublished). Retrieved from http://schools.nyc.gov/NR/rdonlyres/2711181C-2108-40C4-A7F8-76F243C9B910/0/DOKFourContentAreas.pdf

Webb, N. (2007). Issues related to judging the alignment of curriculum standards and assessments. *Applied Measurement in Education, 20*(1), 7–25. Mahwah, NJ: Erlbaum.

Webb, N. (July 1, 2014). *Dr. Norman Webb's DOK overview.* Video of Dr. Norman Webb's presentation posted on YouTube by WCEPS, https://www.youtube.com/watch?v=qFXU6_TYIjc

Wilson, K., & Korn, J. H. (2007). Attention during lectures: Beyond ten minutes. *Teaching of Psychology, 34*(2), 85–89.

Witkowski, P., & Cornell, T. (2015). An investigation into student engagement in higher education classrooms. *Insight: A Journal of Scholarly Teaching, 10,* 56–67. Parkville, MO: Park University.

Wood, C. L., Mabry, L. E., Kretlow, A. G., Lo, Y., & Galloway, T. (2009). Effects of preprinted response cards on students' participation and off-task behavior in a rural kindergarten classroom. *Rural Special Education Quarterly, 28*(2), 39–47.

Yazzie-Mintz, E. (2010). *Charting the path from engagement to achievement: A report on the 2009 high school survey of student engagement.* Bloomington, IN: Center for Evaluation & Education Policy.

Young, D. (2008, Summer). Improving Alabama's graduation rates. *Delta Kappa Gamma Bulletin.*

Index

Note: The letter *f* following a page number denotes a figure. TPT techniques are capitalized.

About the Authors

J. Urdaneta/Urdaneta Photography

Dr. Pérsida Himmele has asked me (Bill) to write her "About the Author" section. I've got lots to say. Sure, she has a PhD in intercultural education from Biola University, and an EdM in elementary and bilingual education from SUNY Buffalo. And sure, she's an associate professor of language and literacy at Millersville University, where she shares her passion for growing academic language, literacy, and helping English language learners develop academic language in the classroom. But did you know she is also quite an adventurer? Her greatest adventure was reluctantly agreeing to go on a three-day family camping trip. According to her, "In my old neighborhoods, people slept outside. When people slept outside, it was not a good thing." In addition to new adventures, Pérsida loves working with teachers and children in real classrooms. She has been an elementary and middle school bilingual and multilingual classroom teacher in New York and California, and a district administrator in Pennsylvania. She has been a consultant to various school districts, the Pennsylvania Department of Education, and educational entities in the United States, China, Nepal, Argentina, Venezuela, and Tonga. She loves gospel music and is a gifted singer, an active advocate for educational equity, and an amazing mother, wife, and friend.

J. Urdaneta/Urdaneta Photography

Dr. William Himmele has agreed to let me (Pérsida) write his "About the Author" section, which serves as evidence of his very trusting, though somewhat forgetful, nature. Bill has his PhD in intercultural education and an MA in TESOL (Teaching English to Speakers of Other Languages) from Biola University. He is an associate professor at Millersville University in southeastern Pennsylvania, where the students find him engaging and insightful and never, ever let their minds wander in his classes (he carries a megaphone, just in case). He is a die-hard Buffalo Bills and Buffalo Sabres fan, which means he's often suffering from acute bouts of weight gain and depression, for which he is highly medicated during the months of February (the Super Bowl) and June (the Stanley Cup). He is a former ESL teacher and speech pathologist in New York and California. He has been a presenter and an educational consultant for various school districts and educational projects in the United States, Puerto Rico, South Africa, The United Arab Emirates, Chile, Nepal, Thailand, Korea, China, Venezuela, Fiji, Trinidad, and Tobago (for these last three, he had to be dragged onto the plane, kicking and screaming, "I don't want to go home!"). Bill is belly-laugh funny. But his greatest accomplishment is being an amazing and attentive dad. His two children adore him, as does his delightfully charming Puerto Rican wife.

William and Pérsida each have more than 25 years of K–12 and university teaching experience. Combined, they have given more than 500 keynote, featured and professional presentations around the world. They have a website, www.TotalParticipationTechniques.com, where you can find additional content and resources for supporting a TPT classroom. They would love to hear of your experiences with Total Participation Techniques. They can be reached via their website or by e-mail at languagerich@gmail.com.

Final note: Himmele rhymes with *simile* (simm-uh-lee), the figure of speech that compares two things). Pérsida's name is Spanish. It is pronounced *Pair-see-dah (*or *Per-see-dah)*. Bill's name is not Spanish. Bill rhymes with *pill*, and William (his fancy name) rhymes with *trillium*.

Related ASCD Resources: Student Participation and Motivation

At the time of publication, the following ASCD resources were available (ASCD stock numbers in parentheses). For up-to-date information about ASCD resources, go to www.ascd.org. Search the complete archives of Educational Leadership at www.ascd.org/el.

ASCD EDge® Group

Exchange ideas and connect with other educators interested in teaching techniques on the social networking site ASCD EDge® at http://ascdedge.ascd.org/

Print Products

The Language-Rich Classroom: A Research-Based Framework for Teaching English Language Learners by Pérsida Himmele and William Himmele (#108037)

The New Art and Science of Teaching by Robert J. Marzano (#117095)

The Power of the Adolescent Brain: Strategies for Teaching Middle and High School Students by Thomas Armstrong (#116017)

Total Literacy Techniques: Tools to Help Students Analyze Literature and Informational Texts by Pérsida Himmele, William Himmele, and Keely Potter (#114009)

Total Participation Techniques to Engage Students (Quick Reference Guide) by Pérsida Himmele and William Himmele (#QRG117029)

Unlocking Student Potential: How do I identify and activate student strengths? (ASCD Arias) by Yvette Jackson and Veronica McDermott (#SF115057)

Video Products

Total Participation Techniques DVD with Pérsida Himmele and William Himmele (#614032)

For more information: send e-mail to member@ascd.org; call 1-800-933-2723 or 703-578-9600, press 2; send a fax to 703-575-5400; or write to Information Services, ASCD, 1703 N. Beauregard St., Alexandria, VA 22311-1714 USA.

WHOLE CHILD
TENETS

THE WHOLE CHILD

The ASCD Whole Child approach is an effort to transition from a focus on narrowly defined academic achievement to one that promotes the long-term development and success of all children. Through this approach, ASCD supports educators, families, community members, and policymakers as they move from a vision about educating the whole child to sustainable, collaborative actions.

Total Participation Techniques relates to the **safe**, **engaged**, and **challenged** tenets.

For more about the ASCD Whole Child approach, visit **www.ascd.org/wholechild.**

1 **HEALTHY**
Each student enters school healthy and learns about and practices a healthy lifestyle.

2 **SAFE**
Each student learns in an environment that is physically and emotionally **safe** for students and adults.

3 **ENGAGED**
Each student is actively engaged in learning and is connected to the school and broader community.

4 **SUPPORTED**
Each student has access to personalized learning and is supported by qualified, caring adults.

5 **CHALLENGED**
Each student is challenged academically and prepared for success in college or further study and for employment and participation in a global environment.